I0556414

Stoneboat

Definition: [ˈstəʊnˌbəʊt] *a sled-like*
device used to move heavy objects.

Editors in Chief

Rob Pockat
Signe Jorgenson

Poetry and Arts Editor

Lisa Vihos

Creative Nonfiction Editor

Signe Jorgenson

Fiction Editors

Rob Pockat
Jim Giese

Layout & Design Editor

Jim Giese

Interns

Katie Amundsen
Mary Kate DeJardin

Cover Art

Individuality of Death © Tyler Holman

Stoneboat 4-2 ©2014

We accept electronic or hard copy submissions of 3-5 unpublished poems, prose pieces of up to 5000 words, and b. & w. art. Submissions are accepted through our online submission manager, www.stoneboat.submishmash.com. We no longer accept submissions via e-mail. Send hard copy with an SASE to Signe Jorgenson, c/o General Studies Division, Lakeland College, PO Box 359, Sheboygan, WI, 53082. We will accept submissions for the Fall 2014 issue until August 1, 2014.

Subscriptions, information, and T-shirts available at www.stoneboatwi.com.

→ Indicates no stanza break

Dedicated to independent thought

Poetry

Poetry (continued)

Fiction

Creative Nonfiction

Art

Interview and Book Review

Above It All

Charles Finn

At night the great carapace of sky
Extinguished, a salt shaker of stars

Spilled, moonlight slipping through
Sprung branches, a pale

Poultice of light on the ground.
There are owls and foxes

The sea on the prowl, deer bedded down
The jazz songs of coyotes.

Did you ever stop to wonder
If we have it all wrong?

Why the geese fly south in the winter
Make those spelling mistakes in the clouds?

Maybe it's not about breeding grounds
Magnetic pulls, or warmer climates at all.

Light Reading

Loren Sundlee

Where our neighbors got them
I don't know.
Books were among the things
never seen in their house or ours—
along with running water,
insulated walls
and regular pay checks.

But the books appeared,
bound with mold,
pages compressed
like rings of old trees,
print small and impenetrable.
Of the actual authors
I have no idea.
So I will say Gibbon, Milton,
Darwin (possibly a first edition).
What to do with them?

We kids had our own sense
of density. While one cradled
the .22 rifle two of us
hefted the box out into a field
where we stacked the books on end
as if a farmer might stop
for some light reading between
rounds of spreading manure.

We didn't know how many
it would take,
so we banked three or four
back to back,
buttressed by others
stacked flat like insulation
from ignorance.

We paced a safe distance,
fired and ran to our kill,
became speed readers,
traced the hole
like the plot of a pot boiler,
discarded one,
and halfway through the second
found the exhausted lead,
its nose blunted
from falling asleep reading.

We extolled the logic
of bullets, scanned the hole
with our fingertips,
one more eternal question
answered.

I picked up the first book,
held it to the sky,
a telescope to peer
into another universe,
and must have sighted there
a small truth of light
through its dead center
where words could be hooked,
hung and cured.

Northwoods Metamorphoses

Timothy Walsh

Imagine the leaves on the trees were basically the same
except that each leaf weighed, say, five pounds.
Imagine the terror each autumn would bring—
leaves crashing down on roofs, landing with a thud,
      smashing sidewalks, cracking heads, squashing squirrels,
obliterating windshields, falling like cannon shot
      into rivers, streams, and lakes.
No gentle fluttering of weightless, butterfly-like shapes
      wafting and lilting the wind,
but solid wedges plunking down like chunks of cement.
Imagine the now-pleasant chore of raking leaves—how we'd
      strain to lift each five-pound leaf into a wagon
or wheelbarrow, stack them like bricks along the street
      for city crews to come and get.

Imagine if the five-pound leaves on the trees
      were otherwise the same
but were made of something like meat—
choice steaks falling from the sky—
maples tasting of beef, oaks of pork—
collecting the leaves to marinate and season,
      broiled to perfection.
Imagine that these falling, five-pound leaves
      were what sustained us—
how we'd ache for the coming of fall, mouth watering
      at the thought,
watching the changing leaves as we watch ripening
      apples or raspberries.

Imagine if the five-pound, meat-like leaves of the trees
        were basically the same,
except that they came alive as they fell,
sprouting legs and feet, snouts and faces
        as they plummeted to earth,
scurrying off as they hit the ground to hide
        from the legions of blaze-orange hunters
and their barking, leaf-sniffing dogs.
Imagine the glorious October leaf-hunting season,
the forests alive with fleet-footed leaves,
        wily as raccoons, playful as otters,
the distant pop of guns, the smoke of wistful campfires,
hunters tracking catalpa, ash, hickory,
        freezers full of leaf-mulch sausage.

Now imagine that the five-pound, meat-like leaves of the trees
        that came alive as they fell
were basically the same—
basically the same as, say, your own hands,
        pointed and veined,
attached to branch-like arms and trunk-like torso,
your feet tethered to deep subterranean roots,
yourself standing tall in the breeze under
        a benevolent blue sky,
your clothes woven of gnarled bark,
birds settling on your branches,
nesting in your hair.

There. Now imagine.

Men in Trees II

W. Jack Savage

Snow Plows

Marvin Shackelford

You love the summer of rust
drawing sweat from plows lined behind
the Armory fence. You talk of jumping
the razor wire holding them together,
and I'm unsure how to answer.
My lips are buried snow, and it's hopeless.

Sometimes while we eat lunch in the vacant
lot next door, guardsmen will work a hose
along their charges, keeping them always
prepared for unimaginable
seasons. Perspiration darkly bleeds
the hollows of your shirt, and you say
with the conviction of a guerilla
just once you'd like to move heaven and earth
freely and by no order.

The Safe Escape of Bears

Jennifer Audette

Each horn blast jumped me a little. The cars would be about fifty feet off and then they'd lay into it, honking away. Maybe people were saying hello. I smiled and waved like they were old friends. The way the sun hit the windows, I couldn't tell if anyone smiled back.

I walked along listening to Richard Simmons' *Sweatin' to the Oldies*. Ma gave me the tape a few months back after my doctor suggested that at twenty-seven I should think about getting out of the house. Ma thought she meant I needed fresh air, more exercise. "Here ya go, Ursula. Daddy transferred my exercise videos onto cassette for you." She'd even dug up the old Walkman. "Don't go past the top of the hill. If you're not back in an hour, we're coming to find you."

I counted every car that honked. At the third, I stopped waving. At the fifth, I flipped the bird. Richard Simmons shouted a blue streak of fitness into my ears as I trudged up the hill and kept my eyes on the rubber toes of my sneakers.

All the fuss made sense when I got around the bend at the top of the hill. A bear sat in the ditch holding a hive in its lap. Bees swarmed the air, bounced off its face and ears. The bear looked up from its prize, eyes like glazed buttons. Its nose quivered for my scent, strands of honey hanging down. I sniffed, too, and smelled wet fur mixed with stirred-up sweetness.

"That's quite an afternoon treat," I said.

I'd only ever seen a bear on TV, before digital came through last year and the rabbit ears stopped working. I knew enough not to run. I tried not to seem scared; animals can sense that kind of thing.

The bear's fur rolled in waves the color of cinnamon and licorice. My brother Arthur, his hair was the same color. It looked right at me, snorted, and shook its head, like he wanted me to get lost. I heard Ma and Daddy in my head telling me to head for home.

The bear went back to devouring the hive without a care in the world for all those stinging bees. It lapped up honey and chewed through the waxy comb. I crossed to the far side of the road and kept going.

"To lose weight you have to love yourself!" Richard Simmons hollered into my ears.

On the way back I stepped off the road to push through clumps of pussy willows heavy with homeless bees. The grass nearby was matted in the shape of a bear's behind. Pieces of hive littered the ditch. I could still smell honey. "Hello?" I called into the forest. But the bear was long gone, just like my brother. I yanked Richard Simmons' hand-on-hips step-kicks off my ears and tossed him into the ditch.

Ma and Daddy sat in the dark living room watching videos of the old sitcom *Murphy Brown*. The tracking was so far gone that the fuzzy horizontal lines never went away. "Don't need no digital. Nothin' wrong with the old stuff." That's what they said if I made a stink about missing the new shows.

"That Richard Pryor tape working out?" Ma asked.

"Simmons, Ma. Richard Simmons."

Daddy sawed logs while Ma laughed along with the TV audience. Without the hint, I don't think she'd know what was funny.

"I saw a bear eating honey on the side of the road. I think it was Arthur," I said.

"Did Dr. Whatsit tell you to talk that kind of nonsense? Goddamn therapy crap," Ma said.

My doctor was Indian—dot, not feather. Ma called her Whatsit because she couldn't say Karadigudda. Back in February I went outside without any clothes—late enough so it was dark—and sat down in the snow and waited for everything to stop. I was so tired. Ma, I want a friend; Ma, I want Arthur back; Ma, I want a boyfriend; Ma, I want a job. No, no, NO, you can't! When they found me, Daddy said I was like a pork chop ready for the deep freeze. They took me to the hospital. To get me home and keep me there, I had to meet with Dr. K once a week for two months. Ma and Daddy were so worried about losing me, too, that they'd agreed. She'd given me her card. I kept it with me all the time in a pocket where I could run my fingers over the bumps of her name and number.

I left Ma and Daddy with *Murphy Brown* and went to see if we still had any honey. I found it in the pantry behind an expired box of pink diet sugar packets. Hot water loosened the stuck lid. Old bits of Arthur's bread and peanut butter floated in the jar. He was the one who ate honey, who dunked his toast right in. He'd laugh to see how I dug in now, without a spoon, using my fingers like that bear. The honey was crystallized but still soft like butter left out on the counter. I dipped my fingers again. I imagined a buzz of bees tapping against my head. Go, go, go.

The night before Arthur left, he'd come into my room. He was seventeen; I was seven. I pretended to be asleep. I didn't know he'd be gone in the morning. "Get out before they fuck you up," he'd whispered. The f-word made my heart pound and I had to squeeze my eyes tight to stay asleep. He kissed the top of my head. In the morning, I could still smell his knock-off cologne. It took two weeks for Ma to notice that I'd stopped washing my hair. She wrestled me into the shower, clothes and all, and sudsed away the last of Arthur with a handful of green shampoo.

Ma dreamed that he came back to burn down the house. None of us escaped. It was all she talked about for weeks. We lived way out of town in an apartment over a two-car garage, a long drop to the ground. After Ma's dream, every room got its own stow-away ladder—SafeEscape, off late-night TV—even the pantry. It was still parked there on the shelf next to the tin of my favorite pink wafer crèmes. I drew my name in the dust on top of the box. Daddy had put his foot down about family fire drills. "Let's not be hysterical, Maude," he'd said. My room didn't have a ladder anymore, or a door either. They'd taken both away years ago after Ma heard me banging into the side of the house one night, too scared to climb back up or keep going down.

"Ursula?" Daddy shuffled into the kitchen.

I stayed in the pantry and shut the door. Dr. Karadigguda said I should try to find a private space in our house. "You need to establish boundaries," she said. The pantry was all I had. Without the window, it would've been lousy—too claustrophobic, stinky like the sprouted potatoes. What's the point of a hiding place that makes you want to leave? I could reach the light chain without a jump now, but only my rear end fit into the back cupboard, not my whole body like when I was a kid. I wedged onto the low shelf, legs stretched all the way to the door.

"Urs?"

It looked dark enough to be dinnertime. A pantry moth flew around my head. I caught it on the first try.

"She's in there again?" Ma was there too. She opened cupboards, rattled pans. The range clicked into action, probably to boil water for mac and cheese.

"At least she's safe," Daddy said into the crack between the door and the woodwork so I'd be sure to hear him.

"Ursula, come out here."

I stayed put, bent in half with my legs falling asleep and my feet blocked against the door.

"Ursula. Now."

"I'm leaving." My lips moved but no sound came out. Where would I go? What would I do? Maybe they'd hire me at the pet store where people brought their dogs and cats, even guinea pigs, to shop. I'd seen the ads on TV. I'd make friends with my coworkers. After our shift, over burgers and beers, we'd joke about crazy cat ladies and pugs that peed in aisle three. I'd never had a beer before. Maybe someone would know about Arthur. "I'm leaving," I said.

"What'd you say?" Daddy asked.

"Who's she talking to in there? I need the onions. Tell her I need the onions," Ma said, like I couldn't hear her. The onions had pale green shoots pushing up from their middles, looking for light like the potatoes. As if she needed onions!

"I said I'm leaving."

"She says she's leaving," Daddy told Ma.

"Well, she's got to come out if she's gonna leave." Ma's slippers shuffled over to the pantry. I pressed my feet hard against the bottom of the door.

"So, you mean it this time?" She rattled the doorknob. I pushed harder. "What'll you do for work? Who's gonna take care of you, Ursula? You can't even drive!" she shouted.

I covered my ears. But Ma was right; I didn't know how to drive. I didn't know a lot of things. After Arthur left, they stopped sending me to first grade. They called it homeschooling, but I never got any kind of diploma. I felt in my pocket for Dr. K's card and flicked the last square edge back and forth, into a soft flop-ear to match the other three.

Ma's slipper shadows left the crack at the bottom of the door. I uncovered my ears.

"Leave her be. She'll come out in her own time, like always," Daddy said.

"She can't go."

"It's just talk, Maude. We've been through this before."

"She'd be sorry. She'd come running back," Ma said.

"Sorry like Arthur?"

Ma stomped out of the kitchen. Daddy followed. The *Cheers* theme blasted from the living room like TV comfort food. *Making your way in the world today takes everything you've got.* They sang along even louder than the TV. I hoisted myself out of the cupboard and shook life back into my limbs.

Dr. K said there was help for people like me when I was ready. People like me? "Arrested development due to psychological abuse," she'd said. When will I be ready? "You'll know." Those weren't any kind of answers, and maybe the therapy crap really was crap like Ma said. I pulled Dr. K's card from my pocket to look at the number again. I could call from anywhere, for free. She said there'd be a place to stay for a while, I wouldn't go hungry, I could have a job someday. I'd be okay. She promised.

I pulled the SafeEscape ladder off the shelf. Blue flowered contact paper stuck to the bottom of the box and tore away. Stripes of yellowed glue stained the wood. We got that paper at Woolworth's the same day Daddy paid $9.95 for a parakeet I brought home in a shoebox. The bird's toenails tapped through the cardboard against my palms. I called him Scritch. He ran back and forth, back and forth, on his plastic perch, squawking so loud that no one could stand it, not even me. One morning I hid in the pantry with him, opened the window and made him go. As soon as I'd set him free, I wanted to take it back.

The window hadn't been opened all winter. I struggled to slide it high enough. The ladder chains clanked and rattled against the house when I dropped the bottom rung over the sill. It sounded more like a torture device than something that might save a person. Glass broke and tinkled to the ground—the garage window.

"Norm!" The TV blared from the living room as the fat guy walked into the bar, like clockwork. Ma and Daddy shouted along like they were part of the gang. I jammed my pockets full of pink wafer crèmes.

The ground was a long way down. I couldn't quite remember how I'd done this before; it wasn't just a matter of swinging the legs out the window and down you go. Dr. K and I talked about feelings, relationships, families. We talked about leaving but not about second floor windows and chain-link ladders. Arthur would've been a genius with the SafeEscape. I imagined him on the ground guiding me. "More to the left, Ursula! That's it! Now lean out and stand up. Good!" I straddled the windowsill and ducked my body outside. The cold air made little clouds out of my breath. My toe found the first rung. I leaned against the window and stood up slowly. The house was huge and solid, just inches from my face, like it wanted to push me away. I gripped the window frame with my fingertips and brought my other leg over the sill. The ladder swayed below me, and my knees felt sick to their stomachs. I crouched down, hung from my hands, and searched with my feet. There was the next rung to stand on and then one for my hands. I counted my way down—seventeen moves to the ground. Twenty-seven steps to the end of the driveway. I looked back. An ache filled the spaces between my ribs. My throat was tight. Blue light flickered in the living room windows. Which episode? Would they remember to eat dinner?

Our road stretched like a black river into the distance. No streetlights, no traffic. Why hadn't I grabbed a flashlight from the junk drawer? If a car came by, I'd have to hide because what if it was Ma and Daddy? I already felt the cold through my clothes. The walk to Dimick's General would take almost two hours. They had a pay phone on the front porch. I tried to find Dr. K's card, to rub the bumpy numbers, but my pocket was too full of cookies. I shoved one into my mouth. The sugary wafers dissolved on my tongue.

Something big paced at the edge of birch trees across the road, like it'd been waiting for me. It had fur the color of cinnamon and licorice. I smelled honey. Bees buzzed—go, go, go. I wasn't afraid. It kept up with me as I turned left toward town, moving so fast it felt like running.

Pickup Truck #7

John McCarthy

I will be pulled over
for a broken taillight.
The cop will demand
insurance I do not have.

You will tell me we are lucky
when he lets us go. It is easy
to feel sorry for people leaving
cigarette butts on the floor.

I will apologize for the solar system
of Styrofoam cups under the seat
where you sit, resting your feet
on week-old McDonald's bags

eaten off an exit ramp. We will
spend thirty-one years suspended
on I-55 between Litchfield antique
malls and Joliet toll roads charging

change to keep going. I will
toss in a handful of lost teeth
and beer tokens from some tavern
named after Route 66 phantoms.

I will want to go home, an addict
to continuity. We will never know
why we bothered to try to go
anywhere. We will always end

up falling back in love. A flat tire
will keep us from doing anything.
My hands so callous from trying
to change it. We will break down

in the middle of a cornfield,
and I will try to articulate
the amount of hubcaps I lost
explaining how beautiful you are.

Pot

Rebecca Meyer

Buttons come undone
Zippers fly open
Breathing hastens
Frantic fingers grasp
what the eyes finally feast upon.
Flesh melts in the sex pot
and blood boils.
Timer buzzes when ready,
about to boil over.
Catches her hungrily
and has his fill.
Eats off her table
till about to burst
and she left empty.

Storm Watch

Doug Bolling

golf ball-sized hail
semi in ditch right wheels
up still doing sixty
lovers in tin shed okay
clothes drying on rack
soft dirt tango
syncopation

tornado sighted two miles
west but already gone north
streams & rivers flooding
at&t down, bridge out
hot dogs, buns, mustard
charcoal still dry

everything cool
child on way.

Something About the Stars

Paul Scot August

Deep in the front pocket of my jeans
I carried the extra key to room eight,
the top room with the picture window
overlooking Lake Chetek. It was easier
to stay the weekend in my parents' motel
when visiting instead of in their house.
There was then less chance of waking them
when I stumbled home from the B&B Tavern
down the street. That Friday night, with Hank
on the jukebox and fifty-cent glasses of beer,
I got my twenty-three-year-old ass handed
to me several times by a local blonde woman
with her own custom-made pool cue.
After we'd slow-danced a couple of times
in the back room between the shuffleboard
table and a broken *Hee Haw* pinball machine,
we grabbed a six-pack of Grain Belt bottles
and began the walk back down 2nd Street.
I pointed out Cassiopeia hanging above us
as if she were made of glittering cue balls
and connected by streaks of billiard chalk
and this woman giggled in her drunkenness,
saying something to me about our faults
and the stars. And as I carried the cold beer
in my left hand, and she the black case
with her pool cue in her right, we held hands
in the small-town hour just past midnight.
And somewhere out on the lake, a common
loon yodeled and tremoloed, searching the
starlit darkness for traces of a missing mate.

Poseidon Near Burnham's Island

Paul Scot August

This entire morning I've drifted off the edges
of Burnham's Island, and not a single fish
has blessed me with its taste for a treble hook.
This may be considered poor luck by some,
but my father would explain how the correct
combination of shiny lure, wind direction,
water and temperature, submerged stumps,
sunlight and shade, and dogged persistence
can fill a stringer. But now it's almost noon,
time to head back for lunch, and a few more
futile casts do nothing at all for my confidence.
Nor does asking for help from some unnamed
fish god. So I put my pole down in the boat, reach
to my breast pocket for my cigarettes out of a still
unbroken habit, but come up empty once again.
Some days are like this. While I'm drifting here
on Prairie Lake exercising my casting arm,
every fish within miles has gone deep and quiet,
well fed and rested, the blessings of the dragonfly
and minnow bestowed upon them by some
deity unconcerned with my mortal luck.

Running Away

Michael Albright

I tell him I am running away.
Where will you go? How will you live?
I'll go to the woods and live on the land.
I've just read a book about Indians.
I'm ready. I'm eight.

If I've made up my mind,
we should figure out where I'll go, he says.
We unfold a filling station map,
find Osceola National Forest,
fifty miles away and named for a chief.
How will you get there?
I'll hitchhike; I've seen people doing it.
You can't do that. No one will pick up a kid.
Go pack your stuff. I'll drive you.

I want a sheet or tablecloth
to tie around the end of a stick,
my belongings all plumped up inside,
but if I take one of Mom's, I'll be dead.
I go back and tell him
I need to think about it.

*

I'm dribbling in the driveway
when the ball kicks off
and bounces into the street,
me following fast behind.
The Buick screeches to a halt
before it hits the ball and sends it gone.
I turn and run and hide in the house.
Doorbell, murmur of thanks.
He calls me into the living room.
Lie on the floor with your arm on your chest.
Now put your right arm across your left.

→

Close your eyes and lie very still.
That's what you'll look like
when they put you in the casket
after you've been run over by a car.

    *

Uncle Lane died of leukemia six weeks later,
It was my first funeral. He was thirty-two.
When my mom walked me up to see him,
I heard someone say how nice he looked,
but I thought he looked like a wax museum
dummy in a blue suit I'd never seen before,
left arm over his chest, right crossed over left,
and I wondered if he knew what hit him,
and if he saw it coming, and why,
when he had the chance,
he didn't run away.

The Spontaneity of Grief

Amie Heasley

My phone rang during the part when Leonardo DiCaprio's character answers a call from a dead man's phone. (Moments earlier, the mob had tossed Martin Sheen's character, the chief of police and owner of said phone, off an abandoned building.) I continue to think this is impossible. The ringing couldn't have been a sign from my father.

Or God.

But like in *The Departed*, there was somebody else on the other end, somebody else calling from a dead man's phone, my father's phone. I ignored the call, figuring it was just dad checking on my recovery from surgery. I assumed I could return the call later, when the movie was over. When it was more convenient for me.

Then I forgot and went to bed.

Biological is a category that becomes a glaring distinction when somebody is adopted or somebody dies. I am my dead father's biological daughter, the daughter who knew him less than his stepdaughters, the ones who will never carry his blood. Before Dad's service, I heard one of the funeral directors whisper, "The couch is for the wife and daughters."

I thought, that's me, the daughter, but I wasn't asked to sit on that drab couch, and in all likelihood, I wouldn't have sat there anyway. I sat in a folding chair on the opposite side of the room between my mother and husband. My brother, grandmother and uncle—three more members of my dad's biological family—sat with me. I felt out of place, wondering if all of us should be sitting up front.

Death is a profitable enterprise. According to the CDC, there were more than 2,500,000 reported deaths in 2011. Today, the average cost of a funeral exceeds seven grand. As a result, funeral homes generate about twelve billion in revenue.

Regardless of cost or its effect on our economy, I don't know if I'd characterize my father's funeral as a good funeral, or if any funeral could or should be characterized that way. Thomas Lynch, the funeral director and poet, writes, "A good funeral gets the dead where they need to go and the living where they need to be."

I suppose my dad went someplace, but I'm not sure I've ended up anywhere.

I bought my last car, a German sedan in midlife crisis red, from my father six months before he died. He moved out of state when I was twelve years old. He moved back when I was thirty-two.

This may seem immaterial, but I think Dad was proudest of me at that very moment, when my husband and I signed the papers and drove off the lot in something he alone had guided and encouraged us to buy. The man who had worked in the auto business for thirty-nine years had finally sold his daughter a brand new car.

Before we drove away, my dad, the general manager, examined my car with the precision of a brain surgeon. One of the salespeople said she'd hardly seen him touch, let alone buff, a customer's car.

"That should be mine," my grandmother announced from her wheelchair when two soldiers folded the American flag. Afraid to clear our throats, we watched their silent and deliberate folding, part of my father's military honors, for what seemed like two eternities.

My mother reached over and patted her knee. "None of the red should be showing," my grandmother persisted, her voice carrying. "If any of the red shows, they'll have to start over."

Grief defined by the dictionary:
1.   obsolete: grievance
2.   a: deep and poignant distress caused by or as if by bereavement b: a cause of such suffering
3.   a: an unfortunate outcome: disaster—used chiefly in the phrase *come to grief* b: mishap, misadventure c: trouble, annoyance d: annoying or playful criticism

After *The Departed*, I listened to the voicemail in bed. I told my husband that something was wrong, something was wrong and I knew it, but I didn't know what. My fingers couldn't dial the numbers back. I looked at my phone as if it was something otherworldly. I staggered toward the stairway, my balance challenged like an injured animal on one of those eat-or-be-eaten nature shows. A voice inside repeated "he's dead," but I held out. Dad had to be in the hospital. Very sick maybe, but in the hospital, fighting for his life. No different than those beautiful, resilient actors I'd seen on daytime TV.

Then the stepbrother I hadn't met answered.

That cadence was undeniable. The conversation was too soft, too measured, too careful. There were too many pauses. Too few words. I expressed my shock and disbelief. I didn't hear what the stepbrother, this way-too-soothing grim reaper, said. I asked what happened. I didn't hear what the stepbrother said. I hung up. I asked my husband if he would please call the stepbrother back because I was now charged with sharing the news, and I didn't understand, somehow I didn't hear, what was said. I had to get it right. When I told my side of the family, the details had to be clear and outlined in the correct order.

My mother said my father said, "Be careful. People are counting on you."

He said this a week before his own funeral. She had taken the train to Chicago with her sister and niece. He'd called her right as she'd stepped out of some busy department store. He called her a lot more often than I realized, a lot more often than he called me, his daughter. I imagined the wind howling, church bells ringing, horns blaring, shoppers rushing by my mother on the sidewalk, their voices drunk with pre-holiday cheer.

"Where are you?" he asked.

My mother said Chicago, and then he warned her about being careful. She'd laughed at the warning. He'd said it like a punch line, but his words and melodramatic tone have turned serious with time.

A premonition, my mother now believes.

A month after the funeral, my stepmother dropped off a Christmas present Dad bought me earlier in the year. We never failed to exchange Christmas presents, no matter how infrequently we spoke, no matter how much we hated to admit we had no clue what the other person would want.

I used to mock the gifts my father would bring me: a velvet evening bag, a king-sized comforter, a fiber-optic snowman. I've never carried evening bags. The bed my husband and I share is a queen. Each Christmas, I display the fiber-optic snowman Mom already gave me on my kitchen countertop. One fiber-optic snowman is more than sufficient.

Whatever this final offering was or wasn't, it was too soon for it to be the last. I promised that when I opened it, I wouldn't laugh, at least not right away. The card attached said, "Your dad purchased this gift this fall. Enjoy!"

This gift. This fall. My stepmother added a second exclamation point after "Seasons Greetings!" She tried to seem casual and festive. I try to forgive her. I try to forgive my dad, fate, God, my regret, people who still have two parents, the nurse who brushed off my grandmother, who'd just lost her son, by comparing his death at sixty-two with the senseless deaths of so many young soldiers in Iraq.

Maybe I'm closer to forgiving it all—everything except for that broad-shouldered woman, that nurse working the dayshift who dismissed my dad's passing as routinely as she passed out my grandmother's medication.

"Rain is good luck for a funeral," my brother said. "It means God's softening the earth." On the day of Dad's funeral, rain spit from a sky the color of used dryer sheets. It felt more like his luck—our luck—was up.

Eight on his right side. Five on his left side. Thirteen total.

"Lucky number thirteen," Dad had joked during one of our rare phone calls. Hearing the number thirteen felt like I'd just been pushed from the top of a snow bank in King of the Mountain, the game we played out in the front yard of the duplex my dad had left behind when my brother and I were in elementary school.

Thirteen was the number of stents originally implanted inside my father's chest. The doctors added a fourteenth stent later, following another heart cath, after Dad had complained about recurrent angina. He'd been part of a clinical trial comparing open-heart surgery candidates with stent candidates.

I can't help but question this clinical trial.

What if he'd been an open-heart candidate? Would we have then had that after-school-special exchange, the father-daughter talk where I would ask why he left me, and he would look at me through the same dark eyes as my own and say "I'm sorry?"

It's unsettling to read a death certificate, especially when it's your father's. I ordered his certificate online for my mother, who never remarried and could collect his social security benefits if she proved that first, Dad was deceased, and second, they had been married for at least ten years. I've heard people say that when their parents die, it won't matter if a will isn't in place. It's a breezy thing to say until you wrestle with having to ask your stepmother for something of your father's legacy, any memento that somehow captured his essence.

Dad's death certificate has both of his names on it, the name he shared with me before I married and the name he died with, the new one. He legally changed his name, he said, because the one he was born with was too hard to pronounce. His certificate lists both names, but includes only a single, finite cause of death: arteriosclerotic cardiovascular disease.

Nobody answered the phone. I couldn't reach my brother in Florida or my mother, my dad's ex-wife, in Michigan. I sat up with my husband, counting the seconds as they ticked-ticked-ticked on the silver clock in our cramped living room, and I wondered how my brother would take the news. I agonized more over my mother, who hadn't stopped loving my father even though they'd been divorced twenty-seven years. It didn't end. I had to break it to my grandmother, my dad's mother, and she was in a nursing home with a weak left side and congested heart. There would be more relatives, people in Dad's life, people in my life, I would have to tell.

I left benign messages: one for my brother and one for Mom. I waited for them to call back. I put the phone on the nightstand and curled into my husband's body.

I waited and felt trapped under water, without breath.

Not unlike other funerals I've attended, Dad's service was held in a low-ceilinged institutional building with folding chairs lined up in strict, parallel rows. Somebody had strategically placed boxes of tissue around the room. My stepbrother eulogized my father, an expert in the auto business, through various odometer analogies: "I met Gary at thirty-five thousand miles, and at sixty-two thousand miles, Gary expired much too soon." I said, "I feel as if I'm collapsing from the inside out, like one of those casinos in Vegas, imploding into clouds of dust." The pastor correlated dad's life to the Twenty-third Psalm. Every line of that psalm became a distinct and lengthy metaphor for how he lived.

I'm not convinced any of our comparisons were accurate or transformational. They were our best attempt to convey what we thought was best to say or hear, given the circumstances. With two sets of estranged families, brought together with a smattering of friends and acquaintances, our eulogies may have lacked the spontaneity of grief.

Mom said my father would only buy his milk at Wal-Mart. He argued they had the best-tasting brand.

She told me this on the way out of the nursing home after one of her nightly visits to my grandmother, my dad's mother, my mother's best friend, the woman she had depended on and who now depended on her. Dad had been gone three months. Through the glass doors, we both watched the snow and said nothing. It swirled into cyclones. It coated the roof of my red German sedan in a fragile, powdered sugar layer.

I didn't know Dad's favorite color or the movie he wouldn't admit made him cry or what he ate most often for breakfast or if he thought W. really won his first election. I didn't know half as much about Dad as Mom did. But I did know he wouldn't have missed that weather. He told me over and over he couldn't stand winters in Michigan.

Mom had the same thought. She said, "It pissed your dad off to brush snow from his car."

Our ninety-two-pound black lab had cancer. I talked to Dad about her diagnosis on my thirty-fifth birthday. He'd been through lymphoma with a golden retriever named Sarah. Or was it Sally? He recommended foregoing chemotherapy, which I agreed with and had already decided to forego.

While I couldn't remember his dog's name, I did remember my father feeding her a long, wobbling strand of spaghetti right from his own mouth. I was in college. My stepmother didn't approve. My future husband and I laughed. It was the first time during my summer visit with my dad and stepmom that I felt any connection with my father.

About seventy-one percent of deaths are casketed and have some form of ritual or ceremony. Dad's casket would be shut precisely at 3:00 p.m., he would receive military honors—two soldiers would fold the flag draped over his closed casket and one would stand at attention throughout the entire service—two hymns would be sung, the chosen singer would also sing a song by a popular performer Dad had admired, three family members would speak, the minister would link the Twenty-third Psalm to Dad's life, we would all pray when asked, the newly folded flag, with only the stars showing, would be handed over to my stepmother, and taps would play as my father was wheeled out of the room.

"There won't be a dry eye in the house," my stepbrother had guaranteed.

My father's cremated remains sat next to us in a standard office chair. All we could see was a brown paper box with a fat label in the center. It was an ordinary package; something tidy you could ship through the mail.

For decades, the cremation rate in the U.S. stayed at less than four percent. Cremation takes about three hours. The temperature in the chamber climbs to somewhere between 1,400 and 1,800 degrees Fahrenheit. The remains are first processed into fine particles and then placed in a temporary container provided by the cemetery or an urn purchased by the surviving family.

I guess the brown paper box with the label in the center was my dad's temporary container. My stepmother handed the box to one of the military personnel, a uniformed man who would help perform the interment. I don't know where my dad or his ashes went next. He may have been placed on the pedestal in front of us when the line of soldiers fired the three shots: one for his birth, another for his service to God and his country, and the last for his death.

Mom was upset Dad didn't call me after my procedure, not while I was in the hospital or even later, when I came home. He called me beforehand, though, on my thirty-fifth birthday. We chatted about my upcoming surgery: a laparotomy for endometriosis, a disease that causes infertility. He reassured me. After all, he'd survived fourteen stents.

I had a cyst, about the size of a grapefruit, removed during my surgery. I lost my left ovary. My father died of an irregular heartbeat in an emergency room six days later. On the seventh day, when I was in the middle of making phone calls, telling everybody the news, it hit me: if I ever had any, my children would never meet their maternal grandfather.

Grief defined by the daughter:
1.   Not standing next to my father's hospital bed.
2.   Not saying "I'm here" or "goodbye."
3.   Not witnessing his death with my eyes, my hands, my heart.

The uniformed man leading my father's interment asked if a son was present. My stepmother said yes, without hesitation. My brother, my father's only biological son, had no voice or opinion on the matter. It was a hostile February Tuesday, burial weather Dad would have hated, and my brother was thousands of miles away in his home in sunny Florida, probably hard at work in air conditioning.

My stepbrother received three shells from the three shots fired by the line of soldiers.

After the interment, when we were all meandering toward our cars to drive to my father's marker, my stepbrother handed me the three empty shells. He took my hand, put the shells in my palm and squeezed my gloved fingers around them.

"These should be yours," he said.

Not long after Dad's heart attack, the one that may have led to his death over two years later, I thought about the way he clapped when I was a little girl.

Before he moved out of state, when he still picked my brother and I up every other Sunday for an afternoon of shopping or a movie, Dad liked to take his hands off the steering wheel, guide the car with his knees, and see how loud he could clap. He'd crank up the stereo, particularly if anything by Prince was playing, cup his hands, and slam them together to the thumping beat of the music. My brother and I shrieked and plugged our ears. He wouldn't stop clapping until we begged, laughing so hard it hurt. Whenever I try to imitate Dad's clap, I can never reproduce that Goliath boom I remember.

It isn't uncommon to go through somebody's belongings after they die, to desire some keepsake that reminds you of that person. I wasn't invited to my stepmom's house after Dad died. I had to ask for a few of his things. I didn't know what to ask for, what he had that would ease my fear of forgetting. I sent my stepmother an e-mail that said, "photos, clothing, whatever you think is appropriate."

I received a few of his things in a black paper bag from a men's department store. I gave my brother and mother what I felt I could let go. I kept his socks, well-worn holiday socks decorated with Christmas trees and Snoopy, a pair of car-shaped cufflinks, a gumball machine designed to hold miniature jelly beans, and a set of fingernail clippers embedded into a plastic sports car. Did these items have meaning? Somebody wore the holiday socks, but did Dad ever trim his nails with the sports car? Did he ever feel nauseous after eating too many of the tiny jellybeans stocked inside that stupid gumball machine?

My husband said he saw my stepmom return the folded flag to one of the military personnel. The sun broke out on that raw day in February at Fort Custer National Cemetery. My hat and gloves clashed with my patriotic-red coat. I failed to wear boots. I shivered the length of the committal ceremony, my body hiccupping in the single-digit temperature.

Driving away from Fort Custer, I said it was normal, some might say honorable, to return the flags. I'd read it had to do with the entrance. People returned them for eventual hoisting among The Avenue of Flags, a memorial that includes 152 flagpoles lining the main road. Weather permitting, The Avenue of Flags is displayed from Easter through Veterans Day.

There were only three flags undulating in the icy wind, one at half-mast to mark the day's military burials, on the blinding afternoon they interred my dad's ashes. I have no idea when his flag will fly along that winding avenue.

Shadow Box

Meeah Williams

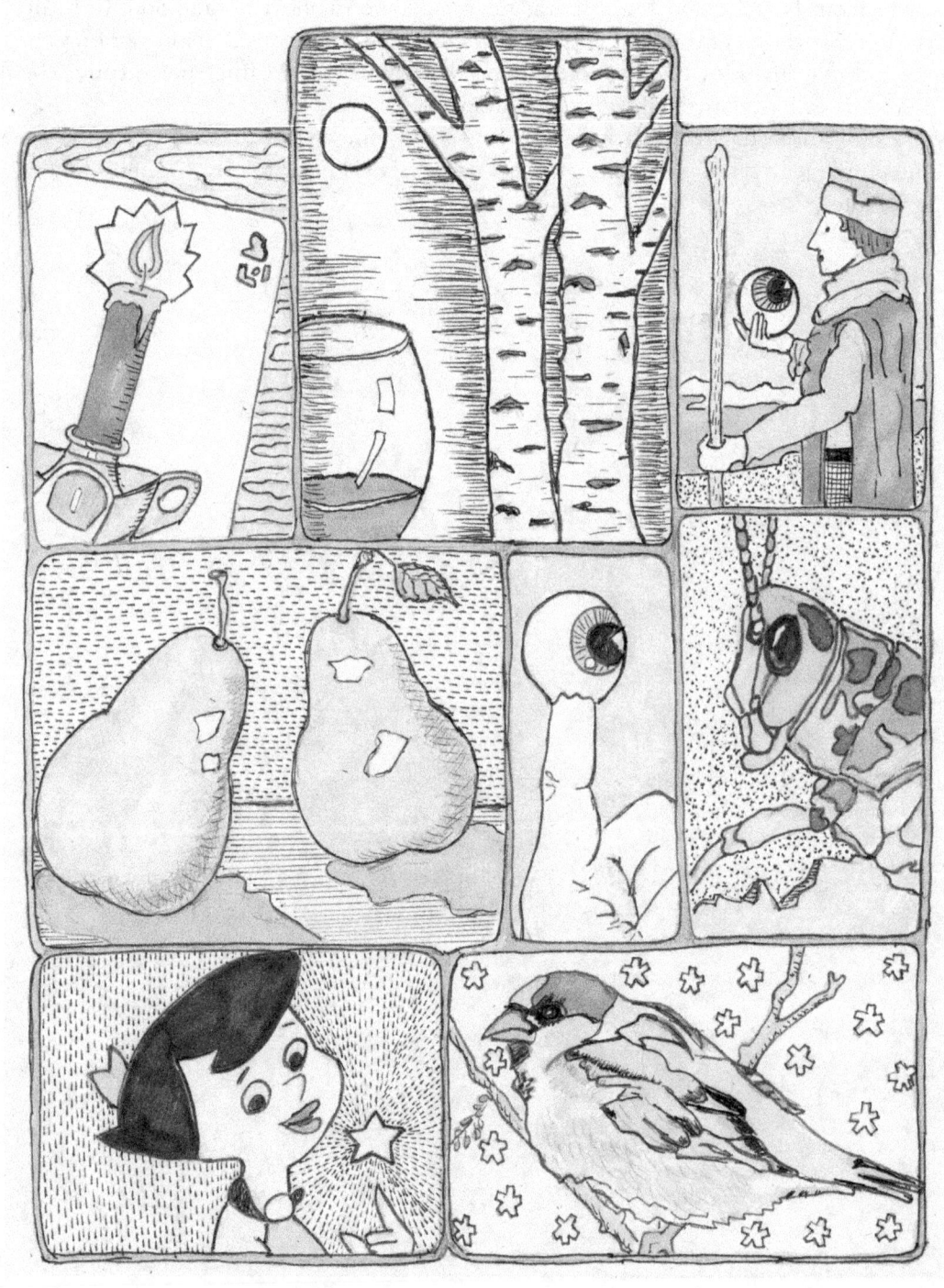

Orchid Grizzle

Meeah Williams

Not

Susanna Lang

There is no river. No trees
over the river that is not

there. No birds in the branches
that have disappeared

into the fog. No way of knowing
when the fog will lift

if it lifts. No sound; the birds
that do not huddle in the branches

have lapsed into silence.
Only the hiss of our passing,

the hollow sound of the bridge under our tires.
You do not speak, either.

It has been a long time
since you had anything to say. There is only

the empty air between us, strands of fog
still moving over the invisible water.

What Spanish Music Feels Like

Gene Goldfarb

All bongos stomping and trumpets braying
bouncing off you in blasts of macho greed
like exploding fruit
pouring out in nonsensical tears and blood
red with rage—one big dare and bluff
like bull fight flourishes—totally insane
executions coming out of black caves.
Try to sing it like a soft prayer but
it grows into a wounded war cry
staccatoed with castanets till it's flamenco
and the floors are getting nailed
with machine gun heels
that finally yield to the soft precise
lament of the tango
where matchless grace
meets imperious youth
and the guitar and accordion
intrude like beggars who knew
your mother better than you did
and boy, it just makes you die.

The Beatles Come to America

Thomas Cochran

Our folks noticed something unusual
that Sunday evening but I don't believe
they heard the world starting over
as Bodale, Charlanne, and I did,
in that order, Bodale of course leading.
He moved from sofa to floor
the moment they commenced,
summoned there by the promise
of a future different from any
he had previously imagined.

(He will in fact tape two coffee cans
together the next day and begin preparing,
hammering those plastic lids with a pair
of Mrs. Walker's knitting needles
until he tears them and his hands
trying to attain the two-four,
which in time he will, falling
into it and wondering, as one wonders
after finally achieving balance on a bicycle,
how such a simple thing could have taken so long—
but that's the future itself, unknown
and ahead, waiting to be heralded
by a song Bodale still needs to hear.)

Everybody was talking at once—
Mr. Walker pronouncing them clowns,
an outrage, Daddy saying they'd last
about as long as a dollar bill in New Orleans,
Mrs. Walker telling Bodale to get back
from the screen lest he ruin his eyes,
if not his ears, Mama twice saying
For heavensake, and once, Law at the hair,
and Charlanne telling me to hush
my mouth when I said I bet you in love.

Rapt Bodale raised a hand and asked
us to please be quiet so he could listen
if we didn't mind to the music,
to which Mr. Walker said I don't see

→

much worth hearing, do not get
the screaming, and tell truth
believe there must be something wrong
with you if you think this's music.

Now I moved my full attention to Bodale,
his every comment and manner
being in those days the maps I followed
by way of forming some idea
regarding my outlook and approach,
wondering if he would defend himself
or let Mr. Walker's comment pass.
I was still indifferent, lagging
behind both Bodale and Charlanne,
who being his sister was guided
by a similar compass and who
had hushed me not embarrassed
as I wanted her to be by my comment
but aware, like Bodale, that this was
a signal she had better attend.

I may have caught up on my own,
have come to the same conclusion
had I been watching that night
over at our house and not theirs,
but I will never know this for sure,
for like so many things I look back on
and can't say how I would have decided
without Bodale's lead it doesn't matter
because as usual what happened happened,
after which I had no choice other than to see
as he saw, to hear as he heard, to be
as much like him as I possibly could.

Well, I do and there ain't, he said,
just like that, like he already understood
something Mr. Walker and the rest of us,
Charlanne excepted, never would,
scooting as he said it even closer to the console,
then leaning, reaching, turning it up.

Camino Real

William Jensen

The last thing my father taught me was how to hotwire a car. This was before every engine connected to a computer, when automobiles consisted of just nuts, bolts, grease, oil, gasoline, and antifreeze. I was fifteen and the two of us had slowly drifted east all summer. Guards had chased him out of an Indian casino in Arizona for tampering with a slot machine. After that it was a week in Las Cruces, a near month in El Paso, and then, on a hot and humid night in July, into a dingy motel off I-35 near San Antonio.

"We'll stick here until I can make some money. We need to get some dough and fast," said Dad. "Then we'll go to Galveston. You'll love it there. Bikini weather."

"What's in Galveston?"

We dumped the garbage bags containing our clothes onto the two beds. Dad fiddled with the television. The screen warmed and went from black to a blue grey and then a Mexican station came in staticky. Dad smacked the side of the machine with his palm.

"Opportunity, Son. We'll get us a little boat, take rich jerks fishing, live off the sea. You'll love living in a gulf town."

The AC unit kicked on, sputtered, and growled, blowing cool air around us. I was thankful for that. Outside it felt like you wore a wet sweater in that strange moist-oven type of heat. Sweat covered my chest and forehead. My pits reeked. I took off my shirt and sat on the bed. I heard cars on the freeway and big bugs flying against the window. The sheets stank of cleaning chemicals. Dad switched the dial and found the news.

"What do you know about fishing?"

"More than you might think. Your old man has been around, you know."

"Been around a craps table, maybe."

"Big talk. You got something you want to say?"

Dad stood facing me. He pulled off his shirt and used it to dry his face. He didn't have an ounce of fat on him and his biceps and chest looked tight and sinewy. The man didn't exercise but maintained a teenager's metabolism. He couldn't grow a full beard, and the patches around his mouth made him resemble a coyote.

"I'm just sick of this. Can't we stay in one place?"

"You will."

"That's what you said about Phoenix."

"We were there for six months. That's long enough."

Dad dropped his shirt to the floor and put his hands on his hips. I looked at the weather girl who told us it was going to reach 100 degrees tomorrow and the day after that. She had big blonde hair and a curvy figure. I wondered if all the women in San Antonio would look like her. Dad tossed his hands up and let them fall, slapping his thighs.

"Hell's bells, Holt. Things didn't work out. Sorry."

"They didn't work out in Reno, either."

"I know it's been a tough row, but you got to believe me. I'm doing the best I can."

"Some best."

Dad didn't say anything. He let out a long sigh. I kept watching the news. The weather girl switched over to a bald guy for sports. He went on about the Rangers and the Astros. Dad peeled off his jeans and his briefs and went into the bathroom to take a shower.

I fell asleep almost as soon as I heard the water running, into one of those heavy black coma sleeps. There were no dreams. Just heat and exhaustion. When I opened my eyes, it was early in the morning but already bright outside. Dad sat on the foot of his bed tying his shoelaces. He wore his work boots. Cartoons played on the television. Drool had dried at the corners of my mouth. My lips felt numb.

"Moneymaking time. Get dressed," said Dad.

"Too early."

"No lazy dogs here."

I sat up and rubbed my eyes. In my daze, I put on my sneakers without socks. I didn't bother with a shirt. Dad opened the door and a clear, blinding furnace heat rushed in. I walked with Dad to our car, a beat-to-hell Vista Cruiser with a dented fender. Our images reflected off the windows. Inside lay everything we owned. The winter coats we never used. A few sleeping bags for when there was no place to go. Some lamps and boxes of plates, coffee mugs, and silverware. The rug bound at the ends with yellow rope. A folded card table and the three chairs. There used to be four, but one had been lost or stolen or just left somewhere. There was Dad's toolkit and some library books from my last school: *The Count of Monte Cristo*, *The Red Badge of Courage*, *Tales of Terror and the Supernatural*. I had not read any of them, but I told myself I would.

Looking at the station wagon and its insides made me feel pathetic. I didn't mind having to miss a few hot meals, and I didn't care if I had to work, but I hated how people looked at us when we rolled up like gypsies without a future or a past, just aimless work-hands riding across the Southwest. Drifters. Nomads. No one trusted you. I believed if we stayed put, then everything would fall into place. I could make friends, maybe meet a girl. There would be a point to picking up a sport or joining a club. I wanted to be able to see a town change over time. I wanted the security of routine. I wanted Dad to stop fantasizing about one scam after the other. I wanted everything to be the opposite of how it was.

"I'm going to see if I can get some work."

Dad dug into his jeans and pulled out his flattened pack of cigarettes. He shook one out, put it to his lips, and lit it. Dad knew about electronics and could pick up skilled day labor in most places. And if he couldn't, he'd settle for general labor, picking trash, loading trucks, and landscaping.

"When will you be back?"

"At the back time," he said, his usual answer for "I don't know." The motel parking lot was near empty. A few pickups with Mexican plates sat at the far end. Weeds spurted out from cracks in the pavement. A lone palm tree stood in the middle of the lot like a religious fixture. I saw the interstate and heard the traffic, but I couldn't see any of the cars.

Dad gave me the motel key and four crumpled dollars. He told me to collect cans and bottles that we could recycle and to only use the money on food. I looked at the cash and didn't say anything.

"It will be okay, Holt."

"I know."

"I've got friends from the old days in Galveston. We're almost there."

"Sure."

"You can hate me if you want."

"I don't hate you."

"This, all this? It's almost over."

We stood there a second in the growing heat. Dad put a hand on my shoulder and left it there. He smoked and nodded as if listening to instructions. I wasn't lying when I said I didn't hate him. But that didn't mean I always liked him. It always felt like Dad separated himself from the cold hard facts. He always believed he could make a quick fortune. I loved my father. But a part of me had given up on him.

Dad got in the car, the cigarette still clenched in his teeth. He wrapped a green bandana around his head and took one last drag before tossing the butt out. I stepped on the cherry with the ball of my foot. Dad started the ignition. He winked at me, backed out, and drove away. Neither of us waved goodbye.

Dad learned electronics when he served in the navy. He got a dishonorable discharge early on, for what, he never clearly stated. I suspected it had something to do with gambling. And cheating at gambling. He liked the OTB, poolrooms, and those late night poker sessions where everyone sipped on tall glasses of whiskey and water until dawn and smoked too many cigarettes. Sometimes he'd win. Sometimes he'd lose. He never got in too deep if he knew he was losing, thank God. One time in Vegas he won $1,000 and we checked into a plush hotel room downtown, ordered room service, swam in the pool, and ate ice cream cones for breakfast before heading west again, to Los Angeles or San Diego or some place on the other side of the Mojave.

My father was, I believe, a strange and restless optimist. He believed in tomorrows, that the next day not only could be better but would be better. There was always a nicer job, a new roulette wheel, a cheaper room to rent. And though most of his plans crumbled before they had a chance, he never lost his temper. Dad never got drunk. He never yelled and he hardly ever cursed. If something didn't work, if something failed, it just motivated him to try again. Or to leave and try someplace else.

Once Dad drove out of sight, I went back to our room where it was chilly and lightless and smelled like bleach. I put on a shirt, switched off the television, and drank as much water straight from the tap as I could stand. I knew I'd be out in the heat a while and didn't want to get dehydrated. I took a garbage bag and went around the grounds looking for recyclables.

After I gathered all the flattened Big Red cans, all the dusty Corona bottles, I walked along the road picking up what lay in the gutter, in the deserted lots and empty fields. Sweat stung my eyes. The wild grass by the pavement looked like straw dying in the worst throes of August. Pickups rushed by sending clouds of dust around me in their wake. I coughed a little. I moved on.

By noon, glass and aluminum filled half my bag. My legs and arms wobbled. I carried the sack over my shoulder as I dragged my feet. When my tongue went dry, I made my way into a fast food restaurant and ordered a cheeseburger off the dollar menu. I tried to eat slowly to trick my stomach into thinking it was getting more than it really was. It allowed me to sit, rest, and stare out the window or at customers who came and ate fries and quarter pounders.

A teenage girl with red hair and big bangs sneered a little when she noticed the bag by my feet. I pulled it closer to me and hid it behind my calves. I knew she thought I was trash. She and her friend, a pale-faced brunette, sat at a booth but kept glancing back at me. They giggled and whispered.

"So gross," said the redhead. They said some other stuff, but I couldn't really hear them. I didn't want to hear them. I finished my meal and left without looking at anyone. Right as the door shut behind me, I realized I'd left the bag inside. The sunlight shot hot and sharp. I couldn't go back and get it. I wouldn't let them see me. I felt stupid and worthless. The traffic, roaming north and south on the interstate, swept by in a roar. I walked to the motel in a daze.

Dad found me in bed around dusk. A black smear ran across his left cheek. He'd stopped at a convenience store and bought us dinner, Mountain Dew and potato chips. He put the groceries on his bed and faced me. I stayed on my back, arms across my chest.

"You alive?"

"Just a swell looking corpse."

"You get us some cans?"

"I did."

"Where did you hide them?"

"I lost them."

Dad opened the Doritos. He stood by my feet and looked at me. The table lamp shined the only light in the room. I thought about telling him about the girls at the burger place, but I didn't. I didn't think he'd understand.

"What do you mean you lost them? Figure something like that would be hard to misplace."

"It just happened. What do you care? And what grown man sends his kid out to collect what strangers throw away?"

"Holt."

"Maybe you enjoy this, but I don't. One of us needs to be the grown-up. You've got no shame, do you? Christ. What kind of people are we?"

I rolled on my side. Dad kept still. I could hear him breathe. He took a step closer to me, and I thought he was going to touch me, pat my back or stroke by hair, but he didn't touch me. He didn't even try.

"You still got any of the cash I gave you?"

I took what was left out of my jeans, the bills even more wrinkled than before, and put it on the nightstand between our beds.

"Calm down. Eat some spicy barbecue. We're getting out of here. Your old man has a plan."

"A new one?"

I sat up and let my legs dangle off the side of the bed.

"I've got a way to fund our move to Galveston," he said and passed me the chips. I ate some and gave them back. "I got wind of a big poker game tonight."

"Jesus, Dad. For a second there, for half a second."

"You've got to have faith, Holt."

"I'd rather have brains."

"Well excuse me. You're the one always complaining about wanting a better life. I'm trying to give you that. You'll love the gulf. And if not, then I'll eat my shoes and your belt."

"Hope you've got a big appetite. Why do we have to go there? What's wrong with all the other places? What's wrong with here?"

Dad sat on his bed across from me. He ate some chips and wiped his fingers on his jeans.

"The gulf is a magical place. It's where I fell in love with your mother, for one thing."

"Oh," I said. It was all I could say. Dad nodded. He stared into his bag of chips. My mother had died from cancer when I was two. Dad had shown me photographs of her, but looking at the pictures was like looking at the models in a catalog. You couldn't communicate with them, just speculate and imagine dialogues and scenarios. Sometimes I dreamt about her, but it was never really her, just someone in the place of her. Dad always told me she was the best thing that ever happened to him.

"Your mother and I used to lie on the beach in the morning and watch the sun come up, coloring the water like the inside of a nectarine. And you heard the small waves crashing in the dark and rolling away. Your mother and I held hands and I felt invincible and I loved her deeply. Days like that never last long enough."

"You never told me any of that."

"Eat your chips. Brammer will be here soon."

"Brammer?"

"A worker I met today. I think he wants to buy the Vista Cruiser."

"You can't sell our ride."

"Afraid I need to. We need the moolah to get into the poker game. We're talking pretty high stakes here, Holt."

Dad turned on the television and found *Jeopardy*. He sat back on the foot of his bed.

"Dad, please think this through. How will we get to the gulf?"

"Why do you think God invented Greyhound? Besides, I wouldn't be surprised if I won some fat cat's Cadillac tonight. We'll buy a new car. A better car."

Part of me wanted to grab Dad by his shirt and slap him, tell him to wise up. I reminded him that it was called gambling, not winning. He just shrugged, ate his chips, and watched Alex Trebek. We passed the Doritos back and forth. We drank the pop straight from the plastic liter. During the show's closing credits, someone knocked on our door.

Brammer looked normal enough. A tall man, he wore overalls and a sweat-stained baseball cap. White specks colored his blonde moustache. When someone talked to him, he put his hands on his hips, and he always adjusted his glasses before he spoke. The three of us slowly circled the station wagon like buzzards around a dying calf. Brammer explained his own car had quit on him last week and he'd had to take a bus and a cab to meet us. Dad rode shotgun while Brammer test-drove the vehicle. When they reappeared I knew we were about to lose our car.

Brammer paid dad in cash. He gave my father five one-hundred-dollar bills and they shook hands.

"You want to buy any of the other stuff?"

Brammer peered at our belongings. He puckered as he thought.

"Don't know. What you got?"

"Got a nice card table. Some lamps."

Dad opened the back and both men gazed in. Brammer pawed through a cardboard box. Plates dinged against pots and pans. He picked up the novels and the anthology I'd checked out from the library. He appeared slightly puzzled by them.

"What about these books? My boy loves to read."

Brammer stared at Dad who glanced at me.

"Nah," said Dad. "Those aren't ours to sell."

"Library books," I said. "If I don't return them they won't let me check out anything else." Brammer nodded as if I had stated a unique opinion. He set the books down. Dad snagged them and handed them to me. The sun had set and the parking lot lights had come on. Moths and mosquitoes flew around the bulbs. I opened the collection of *Tales of Terror and the Supernatural* and saw it was already three months overdue.

"What about these tools?"

"I don't know," said Dad. "Had those a long time."

"How about twenty bucks?"

"For the whole set? Are you Jackie Gleason or something? Because that's a downright joke. Fifty."

"Twenty-five."

Dad poked the inside of his cheek with his tongue. I hoped he'd say no. I didn't want him to have to sell his tools. Who knew how long it would take to get new ones? His main skill required those tools, and he knew it. I watched and held my breath. Everyone stayed silent in the warm darkness.

"Twenty-five and a ride, one last ride."

"Where to?"

"Up I-35."

"How far?"

"To a poker game in Kyle."

"Kyle? That's at least an hour's drive, friend. That's a bit out of my way."

"Come on, all of this is a steal. You're already getting a whole car on the cheap. Now you won't give me and my kid a helping hand out of here."

"A ride is one thing, Kyle is almost in Austin. Don't be mad. I've got to get home tonight at some point."

Dad pinched his nostrils shut, let go, and snorted. He started looking everywhere but at Brammer. I wanted to butt in and call the deal off, tell Brammer to go home. No car, no tools, no sale. But I didn't do anything.

"One ride and you can keep the tools. No extra charge."

"Really?"

"You give us a lift and you can have the tools, the card table, the chairs, the plates, just let us keep our clothes."

"I don't need the table."

Dad leaned in, pointed at the ground with two fingers.

"Then put it out with the trash. If I can't get to Kyle tonight then all of this has been for nothing."

He kept his jaw shut as he spoke.

"Okay. One ride to Kyle. Let me call my wife, let her know I'll be late."

Brammer moved past Dad to a pay phone near the motel office. Dad kicked one of the car's tires. He kept his hands on the top of his head. He wouldn't face me. There wasn't much to say.

I went to our room and got the garbage bags with our clothes. I pulled a case off a pillow and threw the books into it. When it was time to go, I sat in the back with our stuff beside me. Brammer drove along the surface street, pulled onto the freeway, and headed north.

I-35 is a long, straight piece of road, grey and flat, almost ocean-like in its endlessness. It runs from the Mexican border at Laredo up to Wichita, where it slants to the northeast to Duluth, bleeding into Route 61. In the day, the pavement seems to blur with the horizon in the distance, but at night it feels like you are always about to fly off into space and darkness, into some canyon unknown and unnamed.

Street lamps shined beside the interstate in the northern sprawl of San Antonio, but then the sides became open land, colorless and wide. It stayed that way until we approached New Braunfels and San Marcos, where we saw traffic signals, gas stations, diners, and hamburger stands below us. The only other vehicles that night were the eighteen-wheelers riding up from Monterey and Chihuahua. We drifted on.

I could barely see Dad's reflection in the rearview mirror. Only in the yellow flashes of passing trucks did I see his eyes. Brammer turned the radio to a golden country station.

"What grade are you in?"

"I'll be a sophomore this fall."

"Playing football?"

"No, sir."

"You look like you'd make a good kicker."

"I'd like to try fencing. Maybe diving."

"You like school?"

"School is fine. Just school."

Dad kept quiet until he told Brammer to take the next exit. We got off the interstate and drove west, over it and across the railroad tracks.

"At the next stop sign, take a left," said Dad.

Brammer drove on. Dad gave him clear and simple directions. He took us to a small general store that sat near the tracks without any neighbors. A large Coca-Cola sign, all red with white letters, flickered and buzzed outside, and this was the only light. There wasn't even any moon. The place was dark and quiet, and looked closed, but half a dozen cars were parked next to the building by a row of cottonwoods.

"Here is good," said Dad.

"Are you sure this is the place?"

"It sure beats Kansas."

Brammer and Dad shook, and then Brammer and I shook. Dad and I got out, the bags and pillowcases with our possessions by our feet. As Brammer drove away, in our car, with Dad's tools, and back to I-35, I felt a cold vibration in my stomach, and for a few seconds it was hard to breathe until I took one deep breath and all of it went away and everything was normal, hot, and quiet in the Texas Hill Country summer.

We put our stuff near a cottonwood and made our way to the store. Dad opened the front door. A big poker table with a green felt top stood in the center of the room. A few men sat around it. Others strolled the room drinking bottles of beer.

It was an eclectic group. Some men were middle-aged and bored; others wore nice clothes and looked like they never worried about money. One man had on a Bandido vest and sat alone, speaking to no one. Cigarette smoke, heavy and violet, floated wall to wall. A short man with a paunch and a rat face approached us with his hands up, palms outfaced, motioning for me and Dad to stop.

"Buy-in is half a grand," he said and looked at me. "No kids. Sorry."

"That's my son. He isn't playing. Can he hang out?"

"Sorry. No kids. No visitors. Only players and dealers. Those are the rules. Can't have partners giving signals. You understand."

Dad nodded.

"Look," said Ratface. "We're not bad guys but we can't take chances. You want a drink, kid? Some water?"

I told the man no. Dad put his right palm to my cheek and smiled. He said it would be a while but that it would be okay. I didn't care. I didn't feel anything other than a type of frustration and the weariness that comes with it. I walked away and Dad went in and the door closed behind him.

I waited with our belongings near the cottonwoods. The engines of the automobiles ticked and cooled. An owl hooted somewhere and a strong breeze swept over the land. The wind smelled like copper, rain, and stone. I sat on the hood of an Oldsmobile. I tried to read one of the tales of terror, but there wasn't enough light.

An hour went by. It stayed hot for a long time. After a while, the air cooled, but this occurred slowly, gradually, and I sweated through the collar of my T-shirt. I hoped Dad played well and won. If he could get a break, if we could have one lucky streak, then maybe things could be different, could be slightly improved upon. All Dad needed was one good thing to happen to him.

I thought about Dad and I knew I'd been rough on him. He was doing everything he could, and I couldn't have done much better. If he wanted to live on the gulf, where he met my mother, then I could live on the gulf. If he wanted to keep driving and move to Florida or Arkansas or Upstate New York, then I could do that, too.

It was about half an hour later that the shouts and rumbles came from inside the store. I jumped off the hood and ran to the front. The Coca-Cola sign swayed slightly with the wind. Men started yelling inside the store. The voices boomed, deep and low and menacing. Even outside and twenty feet away I could hear chairs shuffling and falling.

Deep down in some chamber of my brain, I knew what had happened. My bones and blood already understood. But I tried to deny it. I couldn't stand to face the truth of the matter, but I knew Dad had tried to cheat and had been caught. And he had cheated the wrong men. They would make sure he knew it as well.

A second later, two men carried my father through the front door by his shirt and belt. The rest of the poker players followed in a torrent. They shoved Dad to the ground. One man in a suit and a cowboy hat stepped to the front. He kicked Dad in the ribs.

"This is your lucky night. This is your get-out-of-here-and-never-come-back party."

Dad coughed and wheezed. He lay on the dirt with one hand to his side. The man in the cowboy hat hawked a loogie and spat. He held up one hand, signaling for everyone to stay back.

"Let me cut him," someone said.

"Hold on," said the man in the cowboy hat. He got on one knee and spoke almost gently to my father. "See what these boys want to do to you? If you tried this someplace else, they'd cut your fingers off, Son. I've seen them do it. I've seen a man get his hand smashed to a pulp with a ballpoint hammer. The guy had to learn how to jack off with his left fist."

"I'm outta here," Dad said. "You'll never see me again."

"Good. That's real good. Glad we have an understanding. Now, I'm going to let the boys kick your ass a bit and then your Texas Hold 'Em license is permanently revoked. You have a nice night. Don't forget to vote."

The man in the cowboy hat stood and stepped to the doorway. He watched the others descend on my father, fierce and hungry like black jackals. They kicked Dad in the legs, chest, arms, and shoulders. One man in jeans and a western shirt just kept stomping on Dad's calf as if hoping to snap it in half.

I ran toward the mob. They hadn't seen me. Or if they did, they didn't care. I shoved one man in a tank top. I tried to push away another guy in a polo shirt. I started punching in every direction, hitting one chin and one nose. Everyone else kept kicking my dad. I was all arms, flailing to keep them away. The world turned quiet around me. The biker in the leather vest pulled me away. He sat me down and held me in place with my elbows locked behind me. My feet scratched and pawed at the soil.

"Now wait a God damn Houston minute," said the man in the cowboy hat. Everybody stopped. They all took a few steps away from Dad. He tried to push himself up but couldn't. Blood dripped from his mouth. "Just who the hell is this?"

"It's the grifter's kid," said Ratface. He'd stood inside the store and had been watching everything with patience.

"He's not a grifter," I yelled. I struggled to break free, but I couldn't. The cowboy strolled toward Dad. I could smell the biker's breath on my neck. Dad rested on his hands and knees. Blood fell off his face in heavy drops.

"This your daddy?"

"Stay away from him. He's had enough. Let him go."

"Well, I'll be."

The cowboy took a half step back and kicked Dad in the head like he was trying to make a field goal. Dad's skull swung up and then his whole body crashed. I yelled a throat-burning screech. Dad stayed down. The biker kept me in place. He didn't say anything. The cowboy walked around Dad and stood in front of me. He squatted and rested his forearms on his thighs.

"You got a name, Son?"

"Holt."

"Holt, I want this to be a lesson to you. Never stick up for a loser. Even if he is your pappy."

Then, in a blind half second, in a moment of beastliness, I lunged forward and bit the cowboy's nose. The biker struggled to hold me. I clenched my teeth around the ridge and the nostrils, and I heard the man scream. I tasted blood, sweat, and skin.

They pulled me off and the cowboy punched me in the stomach with a quick jab. The pain bloomed from my gut to my throat and down into my groin. I couldn't breathe. The biker tossed me to the side and I landed in the grass. The weeds and the soil smelled sweet and dry, and I threw up yellow and brown heaps. My nostrils burned. My eyes watered. I gripped onto fistfuls of earth. The aching reverberated and slowly began to fade. All the men retreated back to the poker game inside the general store, moving like bored children unsure of where to go. Ratface stared at me as he closed the door.

I called to Dad. He moaned something that wasn't a word, just a bit of noise. I tried to stand but fell down. It still hurt to breathe. I stood on the second try, but I had to lean over and rest and dry heave. It was hot and dark. Dad's body looked milky, as if made out of marble. He lay under the glow of the Coca-Cola sign. Beetles fluttered through and around the gleam. The sounds of the freeway were in the distance. I stumbled toward Dad and helped him up. He draped one arm across my shoulders.

"Let's get out of here," he said.

"We'll get into town, wash you up, call a cab."

"No."

"No?"

"Screw these guys," Dad said. "Let's leave in style."

He raised one hand, wobbly and shaky, like a drive-in picture mummy, and pointed at the row of cars by the cottonwoods. Dad tried to smile, but his lips split and bled. One eye had already swollen shut.

"Yeah," I said. "Screw 'em."

I found an unlocked Mustang. Dad leaned against the Datsun next to it. I threw our things in the back. Dad told me what to do.

"If you have a flathead, you can tap that into the ignition and use that. But you'll have to do things the long way tonight."

"I'm listening."

"Pull off the access cover under the steering wheel. Now find the wires."

Dad went on. He spoke to me and gave me instructions that were easy to follow. I took the red wires, stripped them as best I could with my pocketknife, and twisted them together to start the electricity. Once I did that, the radio came on and played R&B. I had some trouble with the ignition wire in the dark, but once I touched it to the red wires, I heard the engine turn and I felt a warm wave of peace. Dad told me to rev it so it wouldn't stall. He hobbled around the hood.

I knew we would have to ditch the car pretty soon. I told myself we were just borrowing it as I helped Dad get in. He grunted and pawed at his ribs. I got behind the wheel, shifted gears, and drove away.

"Are you okay? Do you need to go to a hospital?"

"No. I'm good. Just tired." Dad took off his green bandanna. His hair looked thin and matted down. "Let's get to Galveston. Just go until you hit saltwater. God, I'm tired."

"It's okay. Take a nap. When you wake up we'll be at the beach."

"Yeah. That sounds nice."

Dad leaned against his door. He went quiet. The radio played Sam Cooke as I came back into town. Everything was closed. I followed the signs to get to the freeway.

"Dad, what's the best way to Galveston?"

Dad didn't say anything. He was resting. I was sure I could find our way. Dad would love to smell the sea again. I pulled onto I-35, but I couldn't tell where I was heading.

Post-Punk

Robert L. Penick

In the end, that is what we got:
The end. Nothing more, nothing less.
A faulty coda, a stop sign saying

"No more beyond this point," then
rooms without walls, corridors
leading back to themselves.

We talked about our history,
invented theory, took side gigs
air-brushing T-shirts at the mall,

shaved our heads when hairlines
receded, diversified our portfolios
when the boom times passed.

Later we smirked at the young:
Their dyed hair and tribal piercings.
"Been there, done that," we wheezed.

At 45

John Grey

I'm on the couch
listless and restless

watching a movie
I've seen twice before

while the kids
loudly kill aliens upstairs

and outside
rain falls as steady

as an accountant
at his books

when young,
I traveled widely,
and wildly too I must confess,
overseas
on pennies a day,
all continents
except Antarctica…
searching, searching.

and please don't tell me
that now I've found it

I've found a couch

and a movie for the third time

and kids saving
an imaginary world
from an even more imaginary enemy

and I've found rain
steady rain
and yes,
weekdays,
I'm that accountant
and it never does stop raining.

Vanishing DC: Building Nine

Wiley Reading

To Charlie

Justin Hamm

If I give you a single rose
the hyperbolic red

of a cartoon fire engine
and I ask you to carry

that red rose all herky-jerky
through the hoodlum-

lined streets of your
monochrome cineverse

and if the lovely dame
removes her flapper hat

and accepts that red rose
and her eyebrows arch

upward in question
and your tongue awakens

and like a perfect baby
you begin to shape your

mouth around "l" and "o,"
you should stop right there.

My God, don't speak, Charlie.
Don't you ever say a word.

Far better if you freeze
just like that, forever

in a moment untarnished
by all the unavoidable

clumsiness of our language,
that first, best word still

unsullied by what lives
outside the human heart

Word Problems

Zachary Kluckman

One man, who is an artist, has two dreams and four children. The first dream of the artist is the multiplication of their dreams by an exponential factor of infinity. If each of these children are a brush and the artist has only one canvas, how much paint will he need to pigment a sky big enough for them to believe in? The second dream of the artist is to find a love to replace the one lost in the first part of the equation. His oldest child, the only girl, has three brothers from him. By account of the blood, he is not her father, but he has spent 6,200 days teaching her the words she uses to describe her dreams, which number more than two. Each of her brothers have two dreams of their own, which are a function of living under the normal curve. The mother, who had children with two men, has disappeared into the complicated math of her addiction, the way her skin reacts to liquids. Alcoholism alters the algorithm of her ability to bond with them. The man has been divided by the loss of his wife, leaving him an irrational number. The square root of two. His heart is a train leaving two stations at ninety-five miles an hour. Calculate the force of friction it will take to slow his collision. How fast must he accelerate in another direction to avoid the collision altogether?

The Lies We Share

S. Frederic Liss

Sipping scotch, an Islay single malt, James Stephen Malone stands among the crates, custom crafted, housing his oil paintings. He feels like a Druid in the middle of a Stonehenge of wood. Earlier in the evening, he watched with fascination as Barth Hannah's workmen boxed his paintings, first measuring each one, then building a custom container, slat by slat. As they nailed each painting in its box, Malone felt he was being entombed. He wonders how he will feel when a buyer carts one away. Is this how an unmarried mother, a teenage mother, feels when she sells her newborn to a barren couple? He will insist, he decides, that each sale be subject to visitation rights of the artist. Picasso's loss of *Guernica* weighs him down. Several months ago, Malone, who would rather paint than practice law, sent color slides of a sequence of oil paintings to Hannah, the owner of the Orion Gallery on New York's Madison Avenue. A week ago, Hannah asked for the originals to see if they fulfilled the potential of the slides. Being discovered by Hannah is like being discovered by a curator for the Museum of Modern Art or the jury that selects paintings for the Whitney Biennial.

The bulk of the wooden boxes irritates Malone. The paintings are so corporeal in their shipping crates, atoms and molecules, wood and canvas, streaks of petroleum by-products, things, stuff. The boxes might as well contain machine tools or bolts of cloth or pallets of steering wheels readied for installation in Fords or Chevrolets. Once the truck departs, the summer will drag on as he awaits word from Hannah. He will pass his evenings and weekends at home watching the Red Sox on television. In previous seasons, he listened to the games on the radio in his studio, half a floor in a factory where hundreds of people once worked manufacturing two-ring and three-ring binders for the student market, another industry that migrated first to Alabama, then to South America, finally to China. One night toward the end of July as he settles in to watch a late game from the West Coast, a bowl of popcorn and two beers beside him, his wife, Dinitia Marbury Madison, will ask, why aren't you painting, and he will mumble that waiting to hear from Hannah has given him artist's block. Finally, in the heat of August's dog days, Hannah will call, he is convinced, to schedule a solo exhibition for the early fall because, as Hannah explains, his rich clients give original art for Christmas and his super rich clients donate art to museums in December for the tax deduction. Malone despises the fact that artists, like attorneys, are in thrall to the Internal Revenue Code.

August will wane and Labor Day weekend will come and go and Malone will ponder how to tell his wife that his secretary, Maya Crowell, is his model. Dinitia had exulted when Maya left his office to work downtown because, as a single mother, she needed more money than Malone could pay, more benefits than he could provide; but the long commute, the mandatory overtime, 'til midnight during the week, more Saturdays than not, missing her daughter's prom, her son's baseball games, the incident with the cab driver, all forced Maya back to Malone's small suburban law office and the pleasure of cooking supper for the kids, then squabbling about whose turn it was to do the dishes. Money, she said when she asked for her job back, is not life.

Dinitia will assume Maya was in his studio all those nights and weekends, that she posed nude for him even though there are no nudes in the sequence, that she slept with him, that the paintings are his declaration of love for her. Freshening his scotch, Malone decides to let the paintings speak for themselves, the parol evidence rule applied to the exegesis of art. When he receives advance copies of the exhibition catalogue, he will give one to Dinitia. The catalogue essay will discusses the strong influence of the Italian Renaissance on his work. Malone will point this out to his wife, proud, no arrogant, that his name appears on the same page with Raphael, Michelangelo, Da Vinci, Donatello. He will ignore the critics who mock him as dated, derivative, as inspired as the original oils sold in hotel shows advertised on television. All this Malone imagines as the scotch infiltrates his consciousness.

A day will pass, then a second and a third, as he awaits Dinitia's reaction. His children will start a countdown to the day of the opening the way they count down to Christmas, Halloween, their birthdays, attaching numbers to the door of the refrigerator with silly fruit magnets. It will be part of their bedtime routine like brushing their teeth and saying their prayers. On the night the children post a ten, Dinitia will mute the television sound of the Red Sox game and say, She's going to be there, isn't she?

I invited the office.

Am I supposed to tell her how beautiful she looks in oils?

The ball game, in Malone's imagination, will play on in silence until, the scotch roiling his mind, he sees himself again a young child holding his father's hand, carrying a sketchpad and pencils as he emerges from the concrete and steel and brick bowel of the stadium into Section 35 of the left field grandstand to sit surrounded by Fenway Park's greenery. And, once again, Ted Williams, the only player in the history of the Red Sox who stood taller than the left field wall, stands on the warning track in front of the scoreboard, pounding his glove, waiting for the next ball hit his way. And, once again, from his seat by the railing, Malone draws Williams and, once again, he stands and holds the sketchpad high above his head like a billboard on the roof of a building and, once again, a heavy voice shouts from the end of the row, Hey, Teddy Ballgame, the kid's an 'arteest.' And, once again, the people around Malone in Section 35 cheer and the fans up and down the left field foul line, the Red Sox players on the left side of the infield, the third base umpire, the third base coach, players from the visitor's dugout, all look in the direction of Section 35. And once again Williams, his home runs thick around his middle, calls time and trots over to the railing. And once again Williams says, Got a pen, kid, and once again Malone's father hands him one and Williams scrawls his autograph on Malone's sketch. And once again Malone tries to give it to Williams and once again Williams just winks and trots back to his position in front of the scoreboard and the crowd erupts in an ovation. All this, Malone remembers, and more.

Now, refilling his scotch, the ovation fades from his mind and he doesn't think about his wife or daughter. He doesn't think about his secretary or the corpulence of the crates housing his paintings. He doesn't think about anything except an autographed sketch of Ted Williams in front of an ancient scoreboard built into an even older left field wall. He decides to write Williams, invite him to the opening. It will be like opening day, he'll write. I'll display the sketch, but it won't be for sale. Not now. Not ever. He knows Williams will not attend, probably won't RSVP. Malone will forgive him because, as John Updike once observed, gods don't answer fan mail.

It continues. At the private preview of the exhibition the afternoon before the opening, Dinitia will position herself beside Maya in front of *The Snow Leopard* while Malone and Hannah discuss floor prices in Hannah's office. His children and the grandparents will circulate around Maya and Dinitia like water eddying around rocks. The office staff will move in a block from painting to painting, unable to decide how to react. Malone will peek through the curtains of Hannah's office at his wife and secretary, both as still as butchered hare in a still life. He will notice for the first time they are approximately the same height, Maya perhaps a fraction of an inch taller. Dinitia will stand with her feet side by side, her calves touching, her body square to the painting. Maya's right foot will be a half step to the side of her left foot, a half step in front, as if she were walking into the painting but stopped in mid step. Each will carry an exhibition catalogue, Dinitia marking her place with her index finger, Maya holding hers against her breasts like a schoolgirl. Their eyes will be riveted on the focal point of the painting. Syllables and sentences will distort their mouths as if they were two friends in town for lunch and a day of gallery hopping.

Now, the scotch pleasantly blurring his vision, Malone steadies himself. The blank canvas on his easel mocks him. He spreads some paints on his palette, red and white, seeking the rush which the fumes of fresh oil paint give him; but the smell is too weak to rid him of the dread that someday, how soon he doesn't know, his brush will no longer dance across canvas. He pulls the skin on his forearm where a cancerous melanoma was excised, then re-excised, and the long, pink scar whitens and disappears into his skin. He is still within the five-year window and goes for quarterly check-ups to have his skin examined for new melanomas, to have his lymph nodes poked and prodded in case the cancer metastasized. He relaxes his skin and the scar reappears, a pleasant pink, the pink of roses freshly blooming. Malone tried to reproduce that pink on his palette, but the paints were always too red or too white. Five years is not enough time to master this shade of pink. He digs his fingers into his armpits and checks himself for lumps.

He attempts to concentrate on the sketches for his current painting, *The Betrothed*, that line the poster board beside his easel. Jewish mystics believe, according to a study of Jewish mysticism he's reading as background for this painting, God betroths certain souls to each other in heaven but keeps them apart on earth. Malone wants to portray the moment a man and woman realize they were betrothed in heaven but will never be betrothed on earth. Although he conceives the painting to be a direct descendant of the sense of wonder found in Renaissance adorations, his sketches are lifeless combinations of studio props arranged and rearranged like scrap paper blown around an alley by an errant wind, then imposed into landscapes painted from location sketches and populated with perfectly rendered human figures, virile and young like models who pose for lingerie or swimsuit advertisements: a couple in a spring meadow taunted by tall grass; another on a rock by the ocean mocked by the waves; a couple in bed back to back; a woman on a subway platform, a man on a train pulling away. Meaningless symbols, worse than meaningless, infantile, crowd the sketches: carp garland the trees beside the meadow and worms hang over the edge of the couple's picnic basket; skull fragments washed up on the beach are picked at by crows with shining red eyes; hundreds of candles, snuffed out, smoke rising from dead wicks, separate the angry couple like a bundling board; dead rabbits hang by their feet from the girders of the subway station; the passengers on the subway wear blood-stained butcher's aprons.

Malone pours two more fingers of scotch into a brandy snifter and props himself in the window seat, a sketchpad against his thighs. He feels as tentative, as insecure, as an art student in his first life drawing class. Nothing works. No master can help him. Technical execution takes him nowhere. The only thing preventing him from being an artist is the blank white page of his sketchpad, the blank white canvas on his easel. He wonders if Michelangelo ever felt the chill he now feels.

Earlier that evening as Malone dressed in his studio clothes, blue jeans with slits worn into the knees, an old button-down powder blue dress shirt with permanent sweat stains on the cuffs and collar, the colors of his palette on the front, he told Dinitia about Barth Hannah's phone call, how he arranged movers, specialists who work for museums and galleries. "I'm meeting them in my studio tonight."

"I want to go with you." Dinitia sat on her side of the bed.

"I don't want to have this conversation again."

"Did you put me in your paintings? Is that why you won't let me see them?"

"You'll see them in New York." Malone laced his work boots, eyelet by eyelet. "I may be late. I don't know how long it takes to box paintings."

Now, his head pounds from too much scotch and he does not realize someone is knocking on the door.

Maya rushes into the studio. "Is that it?" She points at the largest box, the box housing *The Snow Leopard*, the keystone of the sequence. She knows it is. In it, she sits on a ledge surrounded by snow-covered mountains. The Himalayas. Bhutan, whose mysteries dwarf those of Tibet or Nepal. She gazes into a canyon so deep that the shadows are lampblack, the light luminous. Everything around her breathes. The snow. The ledge. The mountains. The sunlight. The canyon's core. The very air itself. On her lap rests a snow leopard, the rarest of the rare mountain cats. The expression on her face, Barth Hannah told Malone, reminds him of Donatello's *Mary Magdalene*. And the way the snow leopard gazes at her, Hannah added, a Renaissance adoration.

Maya saw his letter to Hannah describing the provenance and subject of the paintings, a narrative sequence about a woman whose father abandons her as a young child, her search for him when she becomes an adult, what happens when she finds him. Certain events in your life inspire the sequence, Malone explained, and your likeness appears in it, but the paintings are not portraits. It's the shape of your face, he continued, illustrating with pencil drawings how certain shapes such as ovals work better than circles or triangles. It doesn't have to look like me, Maya said; yet she agreed to model for him and she allowed him to do studies of her and photograph her and, before he finished his first painting, she left the door to her heart ajar and he snuck in. She has been trying to evict him ever since.

Angry, hurt, spiteful, she refused to sign a model's release and they argued about it incessantly, during the quiet times when he tried to craft a defense in Bud Leary's double homicide case, during the hectic times when he juggled telephone messages, court appearances in the motion session, and the yips and yaps of clients who wanted everything yesterday.

Do you believe I'm incapable of intimacy? Maya asked when Bud Leary should have been the only thing on his mind. Afraid of happiness? Does my father hang over me like a shroud? You attacked me in your paintings because I said no when you asked me to marry you. I said no because I won't let you do to your children what my father did to me. Your letter, she continued, was like the lid of a coffin being slammed in my face before I could scream I was alive. She demanded he burn the paintings.

It would be, he said, like burning myself.

Now you know how I feel, she replied.

I don't need your release. You're not a public figure. Barth Hannah's lawyer told me that. I researched the law myself. He's right.

Don't pull your attorney tricks on me.

Art offers no choice, Maya.

Now, in his studio, Malone says, "I have champagne for tonight."

"I have a better idea." Maya grabs a can of turpentine from his work bench and douses herself and *The Snow Leopard's* wooden crate, then takes a cigarette lighter from the pocket of her skirt. The look in her eyes reminds him of the first time she saw *Making Pets of the Chickens*, the first painting in the sequence. In it, Malone catches the moment of recognition when a younger Maya, a woman in her mid-twenties, sees her father on the sidewalk outside a slummy supermarket that stocks its salad bar with leftovers from restaurants and whose meats look as if they were microwaved before being put on display. Maya told him about it over lunch on Secretary's Day, their first social interaction. He asked her what her father did or whether he was retired or where he lived or some other polite, perfunctory question and she spewed forth the supermarket story, not to create intimacy Malone now understands, but out of anger for his asking. He did hundreds of studies of her eyes and face before he was able to combine surprise, horror, fear, and desire in one expression, surprise in the eyes, horror and fear in the mouth, desire in the pairing of the two. As time passed, their lunches became more frequent and gradually he extracted her life story from her and put it on canvas. By the time of *The Snow Leopard*, in which he portrays the majesty of survival in a world filled with death, their lunches evolved into dinners and the boundaries between them dissolved until they became a pair of frameless paintings.

Maya says, "Think of the notoriety when you exhibit burned paintings, especially if your model dies in the same fire." Her hand is steady and the flame of the lighter does not waver.

"There's more paint thinner on the work bench. Third degree burns are very painful. You don't want to risk surviving."

Maya draws the lighter toward herself and the flame dances inches from her breast. The white of her blouse yellows with reflected light. "Burn the paintings."

She splashes more lighter fluid on herself and the crate.

"I'm sure your husband's bimbo of the month," he says, "will make a wonderful stepmother."

"The kids can live with my mother."

"Fathers outrank grandmothers. Remember the McAdams divorce. As for the bimbos, your husband's attorney will clean up his act and there won't be a bimbo within a million miles of the courtroom."

"I am capable of love. I love my children." The flame dances around the head of the lighter like a drunk dancing with himself. "And I'm not a whore."

"Who said you were?"

"Just because I'm a secretary doesn't mean I don't know my way to the Museum of Fine Arts. Whores, prostitutes, mistresses, how many did Picasso paint? How many did he pay to model? To fuck? Or Degas? Or James Stephen Malone? Black out my face."

"No."

"Then I will."

Maya kneels beside the shipping crate, the flame of the lighter once again calm, steady. Her face radiates as it does in the painting and he understands now what Barth Hannah meant when he compared it to Donatello. He sees a halo of gold form around her head. The way she kneels, her thighs form a platform. A snow leopard bounds into the room and snuggles on her lap. The world of the painting settles into the room. Malone mouths the word, *don't*. Maya closes her eyes and dips the flame in the pool of paint thinner. A ball of fire explodes to the ceiling, engulfing her and the crate. The flames dance in an incendiary ballet that mesmerizes artists for whom color, shape, motion, matter more than life. Maya staggers away from *The Snow Leopard*. From within the flames her voice emanates. "Your choice, Mr. Malone."

Malone scrambles for the fire extinguisher he stores under the workbench. The pressure gauge is low and he curses himself for not recharging it. Maya moves toward the door, lengthening the distance between herself and *The Snow Leopard*. Malone pumps the fire extinguisher hoping to coax two discharges out of it. He has become, he realizes, Buridan's ass. In college he laughed at the dilemma of Buridan's ass when his medieval philosophy professor lectured on it. The concept of a choice impossible to make, a choice that paralyzes free will, was alien to him, as alien as St. Thomas Aquinas's five proofs of the existence of God or the theologies of the pre-Socratic Greeks. Two haystacks, the donkey equidistant between them, the professor said. Does the donkey die?

Not in real life, Malone replied.

And what is real life, Mr. Malone, the professor asked.

Now, flames scorch the ceiling and the heat scorches his lungs. No time to wet a handkerchief. The metal grip of the fire extinguisher burns his hand. He pulls the discharge lever and a wisp of fire suppressant dribbles out, too weak to penetrate the heat. Moisture trapped in the wood snaps and pops. Maya lies in a lump by the door. Smoke, redolent with paints and varnish and overcooked flesh, fills the studio. An alarm sounds and water, first a sprinkle, then a gush, sprays the room, hissing as it vaporizes when it contacts hot surfaces. It floods the floor. Paint brushes and shards of pastels float and bob. Watercolors dissolve, tailed by random swirls of reds and blues, oranges and yellows, greens and purples. In a flash, the water extinguishes the fire.

Malone crawls toward Maya, water to his elbows. Fire has burned away her hair and clothes. Her flesh smolders. Her face is featureless, like a mannequin before the eyes and mouth are painted on, the make-up applied, the wig positioned. Her hand has melted around the cigarette lighter. Remnants of burned cloth rest on bone. There is no need to call an ambulance.

Fire has consumed the shipping crate with *The Snow Leopard*, the painting within. Scorch marks disfigure the other crates. Malone attacks them with a crowbar. The paintings are smoke damaged, water stained. All repairable, restorable. He sloshes back to his workbench. His easels, his canvases, his brushes, his paints, his notebooks of drawings and sketches, the studies of Maya's face, Maya's eyes, the photos, everything destroyed by fire. He closes his eyes. *The Snow Leopard* appears, a perfect reproduction. Every brush stroke. Every nuance of color, of light and shadow, Maya on the ledge, the rare cat in her lap. The pupils of their eyes, Maya's and the snow leopard's, shine so brightly he thinks for a moment they are alive, and he knows that as long as he breathes, this image will live in his mind until he transfers it to canvas. He forces open the door to the refrigerator and grabs the bottle of champagne by the neck, tearing off the gold foil the way he and Maya once tore off each other's clothes. He pops the cork, sky-rocketing it to the ceiling, where it bounces off a sprinkler still dripping water, and gulps from the bottle the way he chugged cheap beer in college. Bubbles fizz through his nose. He belches, as deep and wet as the flood in his studio. He wishes he had his camera, but he knows he'll remember what he sees. By selecting details, his memory will shape, will improve, will order the chaos around him.

And, he will paint it. He will experiment with different styles, photorealism, naturalism, abstract impressionism, cubism, surrealism, perhaps invent his own. The surfaces of some objects in the painting will be reflective, bright and shiny as if one sun lurked within, a second hovered above just outside the picture; others will be dull and flat, absorbing all light, black holes of multiple hues. The boundaries where the surfaces meet will be razor sharp and the points where the boundaries meet, like stilettos. The colors will mimic a rainbow, a color wheel beginning at the point of perspective and expanding through the painting. Textures will vary from the smooth gloss of acrylics to stroke-visible oils to cloth and mesh, ashes and cinders salvaged from his studio, pustules of black paint like puss seeping from a festering wound, multimedia, multidimensional. Somewhere in the painting, perhaps in the center, perhaps askew so the painting will wobble like a phonograph record whose hole is off-center, will be a donkey, after Monet, because who would dare paint a donkey in the style of Monet. To the right of the donkey, a haystack, as realistic as if photographed by Walker Evans; to the left, equidistant, from the donkey another haystack with as many surfaces and edges as a Picasso from his cubist phase. In the foreground, a small corral outside a barn, the barn where the donkey winters to survive the cold, and within the corral, a coffin, and within the coffin, a baby with an adult face, beaded, long haired, sitting upright, surrounded by stuffed animals, sheep and donkeys and calves, and arrayed before the baby, dolls, three, each of which will have Maya's face, one at age twenty-five, the second at fifty, the third at seventy-five. Somewhere in the painting, perhaps, a cherub peeking out from between clouds, a fourth Maya, the faceless Maya of his studio. In orbit around the scene, Latin letters in a font last used in the reign of Charlemagne, quotations from the philosophical treatises of Jean Buridan, not translated so the common man will wonder rather than understand, so scholars will debate rather than understand, so critics will dismiss rather than appreciate.

Detail by detail, Malone's vision orders the chaos of his studio. A stick of burnt umber, pregnant with water, floats by, perhaps the one he used for the sketches that became the oil painting of his daughter; perhaps not. Malone pockets it. A residue of the wet chalk coats his fingers, slimy, gritty, like wallpaper paste. Tomorrow, he will buy a new easel, new canvases, paints, brushes, supplies. Tomorrow, he will rent another floor in another abandoned factory. Tomorrow, he will begin the studies, the sketches, the cartoons, for his next painting. Art does offer a choice and, after all these years, he has made it.

Wrists

Jennifer Martelli

I married that man because of his wrists.
They were thick—one width from crook to hand—
and that had meaning to me. Archaic wedding bands
were metal cuffs wound around a bride's wrist.
Wrist, like *wrest*, can be sexual or violent;
like *writ*, a law, a forcing, constraint,
thus handcuffs around the wrists, and well,
violence and sex,
if that's the way it is, and that's always
the way it is. I've read many books regarding the crucifixion.
Christ was nailed through his wrists,
just above, through the tough
sinews, the stringy part that would keep him
up long enough to suffocate. Again, laws,
constraint. And the women! Weeping at his feet!
Stigmatics have been getting it wrong, and so hysteria
can be forced by an image seen over and over enough times,
and *hysteria*, with its Greek root, *roaming womb*, and *womb*
like *wound*, like *woo*, like *woe* seems a circular thing. The pulse in the wrist
is much like the heartbeat of a stray cat, the one
you lure with milk in a tuna can, lift, toss
out of your back yard. But it's a bony wrist
at that, and fitting only for a woman.

Skinning the Bear

Jeanine Stevens

He arrived one autumn on top Father's car, each leg lashed to a door handle, head drooping over the edge. My uncle, grinning, shook the large paw. The photo even made the newspapers. Butchering took place on two large picnic tables in our garage only three miles from downtown Indianapolis. By noon, his coarse black fur was gone. He lay stripped, mountainous, like a reclining W. C. Fields, the heavy, translucent fat layered with pinkish vessels and veins. The blob was mostly odorless, but yet something faint, a scent not entirely unpleasant, like sweat from a relative. I stood in the doorway, startled at the manlike pose, wondered—*could he be my kin?*

I always knew I would end up with the brother like Rose Red. I knew that Snow White would get first pick—*the prince*. Red always had the best clothes: crimson brocade, satin and sequins. But, unlike the prince, Bear's innards held no precious jewels, only mice bones, juniper berries, and fermented hunks of grass. There were no precious trinkets, pearls, or gold hanging from his ribcage or spiny thorax.

Neighbor kids stood in the doorway with Mason jars begging for any specimen: eye, toenail—any body part! My Dad yelled, "Quit badgering us!" I didn't want them to leave empty-handed, so I set up a day camp. We made collages with his paw prints and zigzags with the mouse bones.

By afternoon, he disappeared, cleaved into chunks, roasts, and stew meat, labeled on slick white paper, and deposited in a frozen Amana winter. Mother got a new pressure cooker to soften him up, but his gamey flesh, even a smidgen, was still too tough for me to swallow. It caused my parents a lot of consternation.

By November, dull yellow eyes watched the evening fire: arms and legs stretched to all corners, the scent of pine still deep in his fur, slack body stitched to dark green felt with saw-toothed edges. On cold evenings, I stayed up late, my head on his: *my animal groom*. I held his huge hand, nails still sharpened from trudging over great rocks. I kept him company and wondered which girl married his brother. At thirteen, I outgrew my own fuzzy brown "teddy bear" coat with red trim, like a slim tongue buttoned tight. Fickle, I met a boy with dark eyes, curly black hair and white teeth. Luckily, a neighbor was happy to have the moth-eaten thing for his cabin in the mountains.

Putting Shebah Down

David Walker

Morning of, I ate breakfast:
yogurt, blueberry.

She was in my sister's
room, like a salmon, breathing,
with one eye up, the other buried
in carpet.

I knelt beside her, buried my head
in her fur, kissed her, something I hadn't done
in years. I was alone
and spoke words I won't repeat.

My dad came. So did my brother. We talked about the Pats,
that time she ran into the glass door thinking it was open,
what hospital we were bringing her to.
She was standing there, in the grass,
legs spread like an unlocked tripod.

The ride to the vet was short, just down the road,
me in the backseat gripping her collar
as she slid around in the back of the SUV trying to get a footing.
She used to stick her head out the window,
globs of saliva flapping out, sticking to the window
behind her. When it was cold, we would crank the window down
just enough and she would stick her nose
up to the opening, but now she was in the way back
and the windows didn't go down back there.

The woman behind the desk couldn't get the name right,
asked for our address, if this was the first
time we'd brought her here, then she typed away.
I cupped her ears, tried to stand
her up tall, her claws scuffing the linoleum. She was
slipping through my hands. I could see she just wanted to lie
on her side, breathe, or not. Standing made it hard
to breathe. Breathing making it hard to stand.
All I wanted was to rip the keyboard
from the wall and shout *We're just trying to kill our dog!*

The Long Ball

Gregory Crosby

is still in the air. Beyond the fence,
there are stars & fireflies, & the fireflies
farther off, somehow. But it's the stars
that are in our eyes. Someone who doesn't care
about statistics is out there; who doesn't care
about the arc that a body makes in air,
a body stitched & sewn to be struck or
struck out, like an emptied word; who doesn't
know from sharpened cleats in clouds of dust,
or the dark pinpoints of asterisks, or curses,
or black sox or Mudville or joy. Someone
is struck, knocked out, out beyond the light,
by a long, hard ball, & sees stars. Sees the ball
that came not out of nowhere, cradled
in the grass. Sees at the same time
that ball in the air, still, still, still,
in the air, always in the air, helpless
as an arrow. *I thought my life would be
different. How? I don't know… just different.*
Someone lies stunned, dreaming of fireflies
at the edge of stars, where it is always
night, & something is traveling: the ghost
of light. The long ball, still, in the air…
& four men, coming home, amidst a crowd
of screams, of stars, of fireflies, of eyes.

Best-selling author Chad Harbach's *The Art of Fielding* was one of the most celebrated novels of 2011 and was named one of the *New York Times'* Ten Best Books for that year. A Racine, Wisconsin native educated at Harvard and the University of Virginia, Harbach is also a cofounder and editor of *n+1*, a print magazine of politics, literature, and culture.

His most recent editorial project, *MFA vs NYC: The Two Cultures of American Fiction*, is a book-length collection of essays that discusses and explores the overlapping worlds of New York publishing and university MFA programs.

We had the opportunity to ask Chad about projects, process, inspiration, and craft in a recent interview.

MFA vs NYC: The Two Cultures of American Fiction, Edited by Chad Harbach, *n+1*/Faber and Faber, 2014

The Art of Fielding, Chad Harbach, Back Bay Books/Little, Brown & Company, 2011

Q&A with Chad Harbach

You spent more than a decade writing *The Art of Fielding.* How did you know when it was ready for publication?

When I got to the end. I didn't write several full drafts of the novel—instead I moved forward very slowly, advancing and retreating, one step forward and .97 steps back. So when I'd finally written the ending, I spent a couple of months cleaning up some of the more egregious uglinesses in the manuscript, and then started the daunting process of looking for an agent.

Given that the novel was written over such a long time span, how did you maintain a consistent voice and style?

The voice and style changed substantially over those eleven years. They would have to—I was 24 when I began the book and 35 when it was published. Young, then old. I changed so dramatically as a writer and as a person during those years that the tone of the book had to evolve. Which is a good thing, ultimately, because it improved the novel, but it was also very difficult to deal with during the writing—feeling that all these different modes of writing were being soldered together. In part the consistency comes after the fact, in revision, in scrubbing out some of the worst offenses that my 25-year-old, terrible-writer self committed.

In *The Art of Fielding*, the characters are all incredibly believable. What was your process for developing such strong characters?

Thank you. Much of it just comes from living with the characters for a long long time. In, say, 2006, I was nowhere near finishing the novel—but I'd been living with these five people for five-plus years. I thought about them on the subway, in the shower, everywhere. Eventually they come to seem more real than the people you actually know, and it becomes a matter of transferring that fullness that exists in your mind onto the page.

Westish College bears a striking resemblance to our local college, Lakeland, from its geographical location to its size to its athletic rivalries. (One of the teams in the novel, the Muskies, even shares Lakeland's mascot!) What, if anything, did you know about Lakeland College when writing the book?

Basically zilch, to be honest. Very much looking forward to visiting.

Did you visit Lakeland College or any other small colleges in Wisconsin while you were working on the novel? If so, how did those visits figure into the story?

I didn't purposely visit any colleges for research purposes, but certainly I've been around small Wisconsin colleges throughout my life. My mother and sister both went to St. Norbert; my brother lives in Appleton near Lawrence; my high school girlfriend went to Beloit; I once spent a week at some strange kind of summer camp at Ripon; I grew up near Carthage; and when I was in high school I played baseball on the diamonds of several different schools.

Westish, ultimately, is a composite of those places and the school I attended, Harvard. Which isn't a small liberal arts college, of course, but in fact it's not that big—fewer than 7,000 undergraduates—and feels very self-contained, the way a smaller school does. I think what I was imagining was something not unlike Harvard Yard on the shores of Lake Michigan, with dashes of various Wisconsin colleges.

Do you write every day? If so, how do you motivate yourself on the days when you don't want to do it?

For me it's less a matter of wanting to—I always want to, at some level. It's more about making sure to carve out the time. That was difficult for me to do when I was writing *The Art of Fielding* while working to pay my rent and also running a magazine. And it's been hard the last couple of years because I've been lucky enough to be asked to do a lot of traveling in support of the novel. But yes, I think to get anywhere it's *extremely* important to write every day. One day off is pretty iffy—it begins to take you out of the story, out of the fluency. Two days off is a disaster. But if you've been writing eleven days in a row, day twelve is a breeze.

What influenced you to become a writer?

I think the initial impulse comes from my love of novels when I was a kid—six, seven, eight, nine years old. Reading was a very private, deep, immersive experience, and the books I loved gave me a kind and quality of pleasure that was different from anything else in my life. A sense of a wider world where anything's possible. I think wanting to be a writer just means wanting to see if you can reproduce that feeling in other people.

What do writers need to know and do in order to be successful?

Read everything; write every day. Beyond that there are a thousand paths to success (and failure).

What do you enjoy more, writing or editing?

Writing.

What are your responsibilities at *n+1*? What aspects of the journal are you involved with, and what isn't your responsibility?

I'm still involved with the editing of the magazine, and the management of the organization, but my main project for the past eighteen months has been to commission and edit a book called *MFA vs NYC: The Two Cultures of American Fiction*. It came out in March, and was co-published by *n+1* and Farar, Straus and Giroux. It's a book of essays about how writers earn their living these days—whether by teaching in creative writing departments, publishing books, or some other means—and how money, and the lack thereof, affects our literary culture. It's a funny, insightful, occasionally scary book, and I'm very proud to be associated with it.

What problems do you most often see with *n+1* submissions? What warrants an automatic rejection?

First off, it's important to be familiar with the publication you're pitching. It's easy to tell within a few sentences whether the person pitching is a reader of the magazine with common sympathies, or a breathing spambot sending the same idea to twenty magazines and changing the name at the top.

Beyond that, we always want people to write about what they really care about. What do you really spend your time thinking about? What's niggling at you when you get up in the morning? Don't pitch us something that sounds like a magazine piece—pitch us what's in your heart.

Founding a magazine is a challenge. What made you want to take that on?

There were several reason why we thought a new magazine was needed. One was that we were upset by the invasion of Iraq, and by how little resistance was being offered by American intellectuals. That motivated us and made us realize that we'd have to speak for ourselves. And on the literary side, we felt a bunker mentality had settled in—the prevailing idea seemed to be that literature was endangered, and therefore writers and readers should huddle together to protect and compliment one another.

We had a different ideal—we felt that literature was a battleground of ideas. We felt that argument and intensity were the way forward, for writers and for the culture. And we wanted to read a magazine in which fiction and criticism and politics and high culture and pop culture interacted the same way they did in our daily lives. So we decided to try to start one.

What are your favorite literary journals? What do you read for pleasure?

I don't read many literary journals per se. The magazines I enjoy tend to work across politics and literature and culture—for instance, the *London Review of Books*, the *New York Review of Books*, and the *New Yorker*. And more explicitly political work like the *New Left Review*. *Grantland*'s good too.

What can readers expect to see from you in the future?

A novel!

picnic table

B.J. Best

beneath the wood
you can feel
the weight of the meals
of fifty years
of park goers
at this red-stained buffet.
peeled potatoes, bratwurst
from the grill,
coolers wheeled from truck beds
have all come to rest
upon this platonic ideal
of a plane. sometimes
that's all it takes:
some formed steel,
a few bolts, and the willingness
to endure the ordeal
of bearing your ordained burdens
for life. it's honest
as a scarecrow. earnest
as a flagpole. hopeful
as boarding a train.

Supermarket, Ten of Six

John Maloney

Above the dairy case expiring tubes of eerie lighting are depriving
divorced carpenters of any consolation. They're shopping for one,
picking through hamburger and minute steaks . . . then humiliation
along the cereal shelves: no Wheat Chex. Ten of six and roaming

towards the cans of diced tomatoes and basil marinara. Once they
went gangbusters, sole proprietors and breadwinners, bringing
home taboo produce of potato chips and ice cream just to hear
the screams from the kitchen—*"OK, YOU put them to bed."*

The paycheck garnisheed, taken for everything except overalls
and boots, less than half of what was take-home, taking home
packs of kidney beans. No fresh mangoes, no sun-dried tomato
tapenade, no Key lime pies, no mini-pizzas, nothing for fun.

Like Ukrainian military irregulars, they push past cabbages
in woolen vests and hats with furry flaps, weary grins, returning
from the front, ragged and deserted. Out all day in ripping wind,
framing on icy decks, untangling frozen cords in crusted snow.

Cracked hands and wet socks, serving till their tour ends, pissed
and sentimental. With each advance they risk more casualties,
hesitation by the jars of olives, anxiety at the ginger ale, lugging
provisions through hostile zones in quilted pants, falling in.

Our Very First Gestational Sac

Emilie Lindemann

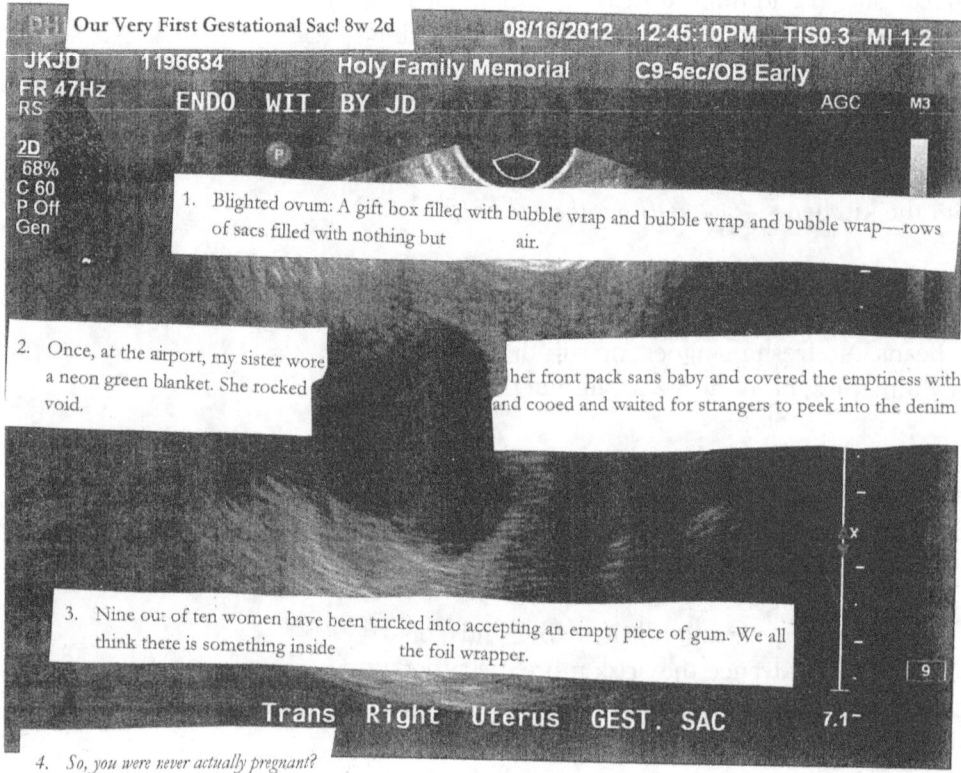

Our Very First Gestational Sac! 8w 2d   08/16/2012 12:45:10PM TIS0.3 MI 1.2
JKJD   1196634   Holy Family Memorial   C9-5ec/OB Early
FR 47Hz
RS   ENDO WIT. BY JD   AGC   M3
2D
68%
C 60
P Off
Gen

1. Blighted ovum: A gift box filled with bubble wrap and bubble wrap and bubble wrap—rows of sacs filled with nothing but   air.

2. Once, at the airport, my sister wore a neon green blanket. She rocked   her front pack sans baby and covered the emptiness with void.   and cooed and waited for strangers to peek into the denim

3. Nine out of ten women have been tricked into accepting an empty piece of gum. We all think there is something inside   the foil wrapper.

Trans Right Uterus GEST. SAC   7.1

4. *So, you were never actually pregnant?*

5. Have you ever finished a Subway sandwich and then rolled up the wrapper to form a new sub?

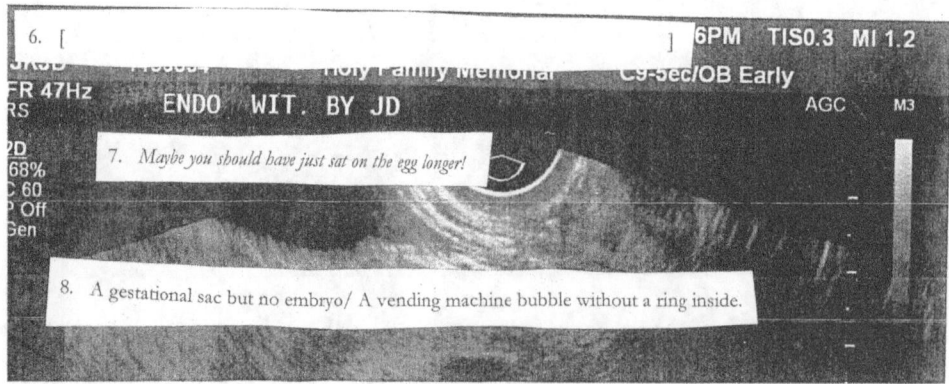

6. [   ] 6PM TIS0.3 MI 1.2
    JKJD   Holy Family Memorial   C9-5ec/OB Early
FR 47Hz
RS   ENDO WIT. BY JD   AGC   M3
2D
68%
C 60
P Off
Gen

7. *Maybe you should have just sat on the egg longer!*

8. A gestational sac but no embryo/ A vending machine bubble without a ring inside.

Preformism— *organisms develop from miniature versions of themselves*

Michelle Donahue

We stand on our wedding cake. He sculpted us,
painted each detail. My freckled cheeks, globed
pearls hung, his gray suit and widow's peak.

We hold hands and navigate the sweet,
slick icing, climb down each sugar-petal tier.
What's important: we're together and smiling.

Let's step from ourselves.

Let's make new life from sculpted bodies.

We'd walk beach side, sand grains hung
as large as dark raisins. Our little clay hands
sickle-cupped, clasped and drying in the sun.

Our laughter had a dryness as if it came
to open throats from the sun and carried
thoughts of fire. How laughter would fuel us.

I'd trace his muscles sculpted.

I'd imprint the happy colors of his art.

We'd grow again from these wedding cake
figures, smile like they do, my dress always
spotless white like soft, new bark, like bone.

Every anniversary, we'd revisit New York,
where we met, use cement and steel to prove
our love's strength, use its ferocity to feed us.

Our new forms would be happy.

We were happy once.

Burnham Park Remix

Julia Rice

Here the Ho-Chunk child walked
the path of work and worship
until the interlopers filled the fields.

Like rival gangs the Irish and the Germans
who stalked the streets of the 'hood
prayed in separate churches.

Two shades of white inhabited the zone.
Within a child the two sides struggled,
the Irish immigrant rejecting her German blood.

Now her child, fair as fresh Wisconsin snow,
lives in the old 'hood, now a *barrio*.
The folk on the street fit well the place
of leaf-flowing trees and crowded grasses.

Native faces have returned—no, not the Ho-Chunk—
the Aztec and the Maya invigorate and re-color the place,
and the fair girl sees the beauty and says,
Esta es mi gente. Su casa es mi casa.
Thank you for letting me live in your house.

Freezer

Susan Carr

She Was Still With Him

Sam Wilder

Chessor Thurkettel's mother, Gracie, had been losing her mind since summer solstice. Chessor'd first noticed something wrong when Gracie'd asked, in an uncharacteristic panic, whether Abelard, her husband and Chessor's father, was coming home from Vietnam.

"Daddy's been dead near twenty years, Mama," Chessor said, "and he didn't fight in 'Nam. I did."

Chessor chalked Gracie's initial lapse up as an isolated case, but less than a week later, when she called Preacher Erikson, a man she loved and feared just a tic less than God Himself, by the name of Pastor Broadwater, Chessor knew his Ma's mind was melting. Pastor Broadwater had been the resident clergy at the Crucifixion Baptist Church from well before Chessor was born until February 22, 1991, when, mid-sermon, he fell victim to an arrest severe enough to tear his heart in half. Abelard, Chessor's daddy, followed Pastor Broadwater to the grave a week later, and the newly-appointed Preacher Erikson had helped Chessor and Gracie come to peace with Abelard's death. Gracie was so grateful, found Preacher Erikson so full of the Spirit, she hadn't missed a sermon since.

Gracie's slips were innocuous enough at first. She tore up her bed of summer squash on the westward slope of her front yard and planted kale mid-August, long before the temperature was seasonal enough for cool-weather greens. On two occasions, she counted her money wrong while shopping at Callaghan's General Store on Main Street, which Donal, the owner, told Chessor about and expected to make right.

But as Gracie Thurkettel's mind got away from her further, her slips became more worrisome. Early September, as Chessor pulled his Jeep into the yard for a visit, he saw his mama sitting in a pool of blood on her front porch. At first he was scared she'd hurt herself, but before he even got out of his truck, he saw she was brandishing a skinned animal in her hand. At first, he assumed she'd caught a possum in the basement, but when he noticed the yellow ears on the carcass, he realized she'd skinned Chipper, her spotted red and cream tabby cat.

Chessor was at a loss. Neither he nor his mama had insurance, so she couldn't visit a doctor without drowning in debt, and she'd raised him practicing mountain remedies—echinacea for a cold, St. John's wort for depression, foxglove for heart palpitations—so modern medicine, as far as he was concerned, could go to hell. On top of it all, Chessor figured a doctor would send Gracie straight to the assisted living home an hour away in Asheville where Graham Butcher's mama'd spent her last lonely months. Being torn from her cottage would kill Gracie quicker than whatever'd taken hold of her mind.

That year, a winter snap hit Black Dog, North Carolina in early October, almost two weeks before the first frost usually bit.

The morning the cold settled, Chessor woke shivering, his crooked teeth hammering so hard he thought they might crack. Frigid air'd snuck through the chinking of his hand-built cabin, and when he pulled back the curtains of the east-facing window above his bed, he saw his yard frosted. In the distance, through candied rhododendron branches and fog, he saw Mount Sugar Fiona'd been crystallized by hoar frost. Chessor'd done nothing to prepare for the cold, nor had he prepared his mama's cottage, so before he even pulled up his long johns, Chessor reached for his phone. Gracie'd resisted having a landline installed in her home most her life, but after Abelard died, Chessor'd convinced his mama it was a good idea, a safety measure, in case of an emergency. But even then she was hesitant.

"The good Lord'll take me when he sees fit," Gracie'd said. "I don't need outsiders stringin' wires all over my house in the event something goes wrong. I been fine for years without 'em."

Chessor held the plastic receiver to his head and waited, but instead of a ring, the operator's squawk blared into his ear. The ice must've weighed too heavy and torn down the lone wire woven up the mountain.

"Shitfire," Chessor muttered. His mama would probably be fine—she'd lived on top of Mount Sugar Fiona her whole life, used to the chill of the first frost—but, aside from his time in the military, Chessor'd lived in Black Dog his whole life, too, and he couldn't remember such a wicked cold hitting the town so early. The elevation of Gracie's cottage was nearly one thousand feet above Black Dog's Main Street, which put it at five thousand above sea level, and on average, the thermometer on Gracie's porch read ten to twenty degrees colder than the thermometer on the porch of Callaghan's. In the summer, Gracie's cabin was comfortable; in the winter, it was dangerous.

Alongside the hoar frost, six or seven inches of snow had fallen on Mount Sugar Fiona, and Chessor had to stop at the first switchback up Gracie's gnarled driveway to lock the hubcaps of his old Wrangler into four-wheel drive. Where he'd stopped, low-growing holly and pine branches wearing winter silver scraped the sides of Chessor's Jeep like bone fingers, and as he knelt in the snow to crank the salt-crusted dials on his hubcaps, the cold raised goose pimples along Chessor's neck and arms. Winter crept under his collar, up his nostrils, into his lungs, reminding him the cold chose to spare him now—and always had—but if it wanted to, it could snuff every bit of warmth from his body. Or his mama's.

Even though the Thurkettels had been in Black Dog since great-great-great-grandfather Eadwig had emigrated from Yorkshire, and even though they were bred thick-gutted and broad-shouldered, insulated from the brutal winters that hit northern England, Gracie'd become frail in her older age, little more than a glass skeleton and paper-thin skin. She no longer had the full hips, stomach and breasts Chessor remembered from his childhood, nothing left to keep the cold from slowing her blood, dragging her body temperature below the safety of ninety-seven degrees.

Chessor drove straight into Gracie's yard. Before his Wrangler had skidded to a stop, he saw the window closest to the front door was open, the doily curtains his father had hated so much snagging in the bright-berried holly along the cottage's front. He loped along the snow-covered yard, wishing he could move quicker, but he'd caught a bullet in his knee during the Battle of Hue back in '68. His kneecap had been shattered, and the wound left him with a severe limp.

Chessor slipped on his weak leg as he approached the three weatherworn steps up to Gracie's front porch, and he planted his palms in the snow and twisted his body as he fell. His face hit the ground hard, and when he lifted it, a blast of frigid wind raked against the melting snow on his cheek. He swore his skin was freezing, blackening and peeling off in thin sheets, but he also knew that wasn't the case, because while he'd never experienced hypothermia, he'd heard you were alive as long as you were cold. When you freeze to death, you die warm.

Chessor almost tore his mama's front door off the hinges after he scrambled onto the porch. He prayed a warm draft would meet him when the heavy hickory swung open, but the air in Gracie's house was as deathly as the air outside. The kitchen window above the sink, visible from where he stood in the living room, was open like the gaping window to his right. Chessor called for Gracie, his voice like grinding sandstones. The anxiety in his belly was fermenting, turning cold and sour, and he worried maybe his mama, in her confusion, had wandered into the woods behind her cottage, towards the stream that started near the peak of Mount Sugar Fiona and ran all the way down to Black Dog, then into the Cherokee National Forest, eventually winding its way across the Tennessee border into moonshine country.

Chessor rushed quick as his knee would allow to his mama's bedroom. Gracie's bed was made like she'd measured exactly how to pull every cover even. He threw the closet doors off their runners hoping, on a whim, his mother might be hunched behind the moth-bitten housecoats and church-going dresses, but he found only snow that had entered through the open window above her bed.

Chessor crossed the hall to the bathroom. He couldn't feel the tips of his fingers, and ice crystals collected in his mustache as his worried breaths quickened. The window opposite the bathroom door was also wide open, and a pattern of frost spiderwebbed Gracie's mirror. Desperately, Chessor threw back the shower curtain, not expecting to find anything, but there his mama lay, curled naked in her bathtub, her hair speckled with the same hoar frost coating the rest of the mountain.

Bright shock blinded Chessor for a moment, but he focused on measuring his breaths, coming to terms with the situation, leveling his emotions. It was a trick he'd learned in Vietnam, and it had saved him on two bloody occasions. Now, it was going to save his mama.

As he knelt to scoop his mama, as his unprotected joint and sandy shards of leftover bone ground into to the tiling, Chessor felt like he'd caught a fresh bullet in the knee, but Gracie couldn't have weighed ninety-five pounds, light as a feather and small as a child against Chessor's Clydesdale chest, so he was back on his feet before the pain became too much.

Gracie's rare breaths came shallow as Chessor carried her across the hall. He pulled back the heavy, hand-stitched quilt decorating Gracie's crisp bed with his free hand, and slipped his mama under the covers, pulling the quilt back up, packing it tight around her neck, trapping what little warmth she had left close to her body. Her face was gray, eyelids blue, lips pale purple, drained of blood. Her veins had retreated close to her bones for warmth, which, frail as she was, wasn't far enough to ward against the cold.

Gracie slept the rest of the day and through the night.

After getting her in bed, Chessor'd moved from room to room, closed all the open windows. The pine branches usually pressed against the kitchen had invited themselves in, and Chessor hacked at them with his mama's lone carving knife like they'd thrown the window wide, like they worked with the cold to see every bit of warmth on Mount Sugar Fiona, especially in Gracie's home, suffocated.

Chessor built a fire in the fat black pot-belly stove in his mama's living room, and he piled precious fatlighter—dead pine logs saturated with sap—onto the fire until the small drifts of snow that had collected on the sills of the open windows melted and dried. When Chessor finally stood and threw his jacket off, his flannel was soaked through with sweat. His face was red as a blood blister, and his dried lips had begun to crack.

During the time it took to reheat his mother's cottage, Chessor kept clear of his feelings, but now that he'd battled the cold, filled the cottage with nurturing heat that forced its way into Gracie's room, under her covers, drawing the blood vessels away from her bones so her body temperature could climb back to the range of the living, he welcomed his feelings home.

Since he could recall, Chessor'd prided himself a lone wolf. Decades ago, a week or so before he was shipped to Vietnam, his father'd told him to trust his company, but not too much, because in the end, a man has to look out for himself. Before Chessor'd climbed on the bus up from Bryson City en route to Fort Bragg, Abelard'd pulled him in for a hug, one of the few Chessor ever received from the old man. "You keep in mind ain't no one else matter in a tussle with death," Chessor's dad had said with liquor and tobacco on his breath.

At the Battle of Hue, Chessor'd learned just how true his dad's words were. As Chessor's company moved to their ordered location flanking the tomb of Minh Mang, Guy Hannenberg, a watery-eyed Midwestern boy who never shut his goddamned mouth, was spooked by a bird who'd popped its head above one of the tiered roofs of a temple across the water. Guy fired, and the report invited a rain of sniper bullets. Chessor'd broken ranks after the stray shot destroyed his kneecap, and, leaving his company behind to be slaughtered, crawled nearly five miles on his belly through the underbrush, eastward towards the coast, without any idea where he was headed.

Since he'd moved back to Black Dog, Chessor'd boasted the only reason he was alive was because he'd relied on himself, which was almost true. After a couple drinks, he'd also curse Hannenberg, growling he hoped the boy'd drowned at the bottom of a Vietcong sewer trough.

Yes, Chessor Thurkettel prided himself an island, but the reality that his mama might be dying a room over split him open. It hadn't been a surprise when Abelard's heart failed. The man smoked twenty hand-rolled cigarettes a day and poured enough whiskey down his throat before bed to get the entirety of Swain County drunk. In fact, Chessor was surprised his daddy had made it sixty-five full years, but unlike Abelard's heart failure, Chessor couldn't point to Gracie's vices or shortcomings to explain what ate her brain, made her throw open windows during a cold snap. In many ways, man was responsible for cutting his own path to the grave, but Gracie'd avoided vices and eaten heartily to see her path was long.

Chessor slumped into his mama's cushioned rocker next to the potbelly. Other than drink at The Block 'N' Tackle, smoke like his old man used to, and illegally hunt when he was sober enough to see down his rifle, all he did was care for his mama. He'd never taken a wife, because no woman worth marrying stayed in Black Dog. He often joked he was married to Mount Sugar Fiona, and that that old bitch was more woman than he could handle. But now, staring out the westward-facing window at the snow-covered Smokies rolling toward Tennessee, Chessor could no longer lie to himself. It was easy to be an island when someone needed him regardless.

Before dawn on the morning Gracie woke, a high-pitched wind announcing more snow ripped him from the daze of staring into the fire, and he realized he was just massaging coals with his iron poker, raking them back and forth so they hummed orange before fading gray. He reached for another pine log, but there were none left. He needed another armload from the woodbox behind the cottage.

Chessor pulled his shearling-lined flannel jacket back on and fought the door open against the wind. Outside, he wiped snow from the thermometer hanging by the doorframe. Even though a sheet of ice had crystallized atop the glass tube, he could see every ounce of mercury was collected at the bottom. Zero degrees. Flat. And he could only imagine what the actual temperature might be with the wind whipping like it was. Deep in the pine forest surrounding Gracie's cottage, the pops and cracks of trees dropping limbs too heavy with snow and ice fired like rifle blasts. The biting cold made the dull pain living in his shot knee throb such that he could barely put his weight on it.

Around back, Chessor found the fire-red carcass of a dead cardinal sprawled atop the woodbox. The bird was dusted with snow, but not coated over, so it must have just died—frozen mid-flight—before dropping. The little bird's body was still soft, not yet frozen, when Chessor tucked the bird into the snow. The snow bit Chessor's fingers, turned them pink as cooked hot dogs, and he regretted not bringing gloves when he left his cabin the morning before. Chessor's fingertips burned as he pried open the frozen woodbox lid.

With an armload of damp logs and boots full of snow, Chessor trudged back around Gracie's cottage, but before he was even on the porch, he heard his mother coughing like she was forcing glass shards from her throat. Chessor's knotted anxiety that had loosened into a thin thread of worry overnight wound tight again, but Chessor felt a shadow of relief, too, because if his mama was coughing, it meant she was alive. He'd checked on her every hour or so the night before, and most times he couldn't tell whether she was breathing, so he'd floated his fingers below her nostrils and waited for an exhale. He hated to hear his mama's painful cough, but he thanked the Lord for giving her the strength to battle the hardened phlegm in her throat.

Chessor hobbled across the porch, threw open the door, dropped the firewood on the deerskin by the stove, and gimped to Gracie's side quick as his knee would allow.

She was still on her back, arms under the covers like the quilts and blankets were too heavy to shed, and as she coughed, her head bucked, bouncing against the pillow, matting her mess of gray curls.

"What can I do, Mama?" Chessor asked, leaning over her bed. At the sound of his voice, she swiveled her head. The corners of her eyes had yellowed, the whites spiderwebbed by thin veins. Her skin clung to her skull like graying parchment. She looked like she'd spent the night in a cold grave, covered over by frozen dirt, then decided it wasn't her time and clawed her way back to the world of the living.

Between coughs, Gracie moved her mouth like she was trying to speak, but instead of forming words, she smacked her lips and raked her dehydrated tongue across them. Chessor realized she hadn't had a sip of water for well over a day now, maybe thirty-six hours. "I'll be right back, Mama," he whispered.

No water spilled into the Mason jar from the kitchen faucet when Chessor twisted the handle—frozen pipes—and Chessor entertained the idea of dipping the jar into the toilet. Instead, he grabbed one of his mama's pots hanging from the clapboard cupboard next to the brown, squat icebox, scooped a potful of snow from the porch and set it to boiling on the potbelly stove heating the house.

"I got water comin'," Chessor told his mama as he knelt by her side. Her brow felt like cold wax paper when he lay a hand across it. "Speak up, Mama," he begged. "Tell me what you need." Pleading like he was, Chessor was taken back to his childhood, taken back to the days Gracie used to have him march into the woods and pluck the switch she'd swat him with. If he returned with a stick too small, she'd send him back out and add lashings to his punishment. He'd beg her to please not switch him, not welt the back of his thighs and his butt with the springy green branch, but she never listened, never replied.

Chessor'd opened the window above the sink and held the pot of water he'd boiled on the pot-belly outside so it could cool. Now, he tipped a Mason jar full of warm fluid to his mama's cracked lips. Droplets ran down her cheeks and chin, but were absorbed by her quilted pillow. The dry skin on her lips soaked up the water like a thirsty sponge, and she moved her head forward to drink more.

She coughed again, spraying water down the pile of blankets covering her body, and her cough was followed by a rattling moan, the mucous in her throat disturbed by her vocal chords. The explosion made Chessor jump, his heart hammering in his chest, but he wiped his mother's mouth. His faced flushed, and sweat beaded his eyebrows from both the heat of Gracie's cottage and the adrenaline driving his blood pressure up. Now that his mother was moaning, simple and ugly as the sound was, it meant she was fighting her way back. Her moan was a step away from the grave.

Relief flooded Chessor's mind, and gratitude followed. Chessor remained on his knees by his mother's side, barely feeling the pain in his blown joint, and he tipped the jar to his mother's mouth again. She sipped the warm water, and Chessor noticed the blankets rising and falling. She was breathing semi-regularly, and Chessor's tunnel vision widened. The entirety of his mother's room began to come into focus. At the foot of Gracie's bed was her simple cherrywood dresser built by Scoot Filson back in the '80s, and above it hung a picture of Abelard. Chessor's daddy squatted in mud by a twenty-point buck, his Winchester Model 94 slung over his left shoulder and a clay jug of mule kick uncorked in his right hand. In the picture, Abelard wasn't smiling, but wore the stony-faced look of pride Chessor'd first seen the afternoon in second grade when Abelard had to come fetch Chessor from the principal's office after the boy'd punched Lenny Culler straight in the teeth for a reason he couldn't now recall. To the right of the dresser was his mother's vanity, a tabletop with three mirrors pocked with black spots folding out from one another. The vanity was empty except for a white pillar candle burned halfway down. Chessor couldn't remember his mother ever sitting at the padded stool tucked underneath, or wearing makeup for that matter.

Everything in Gracie's room was tidy; nothing out of place. *If I didn't know any better*, Chessor thought, *I couldn't even tell she's losing herself.*

"I ain't dead," Gracie said.

"No Mama, you ain't dead," Chessor said, and the words felt truer than any prayer that'd passed his lips. Warmth spread from his chest outward, blocking the little pain left in his knee, stretching all the way to his fingertips, the likes of which he hadn't felt since he buried the dead cardinal in the snow.

Gracie was still cocooned under the blankets, and she'd made no move to throw them off. The muted light coming from the frosted window over her bed seemed to shine through her skin so Chessor could see his mother's skull beneath.

"Why not?" she asked. Her sunken eyes gazed somewhere over Chessor's shoulder like she was asking an invisible third party, and she expected an answer.

Chessor stood on his mama's porch, his hands in his pockets and a smoldering cigarette hanging from his lips. It was his fourth smoke in a row, and ice crusted the hair below his nostrils, as well as the graying beard around his mouth. Wind slapped his face, and black clouds continued to dump fat flakes on Mount Sugar Fiona, blotting out the sun as he watched its withering glow fade below the horizon over in Tennessee.

After asking why she hadn't yet died, Gracie'd asked Chessor twice how long it'd be until Abelard got back from his trip to Gatlinburg to pick up his venison from the smoker, because boy she was hungry, and that's all she wanted to eat.

"Mama, Dad's dead," Chessor'd spat the second time she'd asked. "He ain't going to be back with deer meat." Gracie's eyes had glazed, like they'd been stricken with mild cataracts, and Chessor could tell she wasn't registering a thing he was saying. A rotten guilt had then bloomed in Chessor's stomach for snapping at his mama. "Do you want something to eat other than Dad's deer meat?"

No response.

"I was warm," she'd eventually chirped as he limped back and forth across her small bedroom, trying to puzzle through what to do next. "I ain't now," she croaked, even though she still had the covers tucked up around her neck. "I want to be warm again."

"What do you mean, Mama?" Chessor'd replied, hobbling to her bedside, but before the question was out of his mouth, he'd realized she was remembering how she felt as she lay in the shower inches from slipping into a hypothermic sleep, her temperature dropping to the point her heart pumped only every three or four seconds before quitting her. When you freeze to death, you die warm.

Chessor finished his cigarette and flicked the butt into the wind. The orange filter whipped away, carried into the trees. He put another cigarette between his lips. He had one question left to ask his mama, and each cigarette gave him an extra five minutes before he had to face her answer.

Before Chessor limped from the porch back to his mama's room, he swung open the grated door of the pot-belly stove. The fire'd died, but he didn't bother throwing fresh logs on. Gracie'd taken to moaning again, the echo of which chilled Chessor more than the winter weather.

Gracie's gray hair had matted close to her head like a pelt, and her red quilted pillow had swallowed her head to the ears. Barely any light filtered through the window above her bed, so Chessor struck one of the kitchen matches he used for his cigarettes, held the flame to the wick, and set the pillar candle on her bedside table once it was lit. The flickering light danced off the wrinkles Gracie'd collected over her years. Her eyes were sunk so deep the shadowed sockets looked empty.

"Mama," Chessor said. "Look at me if you can hear me." He lifted the candle from the table and held it close enough to her face to trace her line of sight. She stared ahead, towards the picture of Abelard with his buck and his moonshine. "Mama," Chessor said again louder, and when she didn't answer, something snagged in his throat. Gracie's eyes stayed glue to her husband.

Chessor knew he didn't need to ask his mama whether she knew who he—her son—was, so he began peeling the covers from her bed. He folded them as he lifted one after another, stacking them by her bedside. The snag in his throat expanded, and for the first time since bullets went whizzing by through the underbrush of Vietnamese jungle, Chessor Thurkettel felt fear. It wasn't fear for his life, though. He'd figured out long ago living was much more difficult than its corollary. He feared loneliness, living without anyone to love him or love back. It was fear that he'd have feelings unspeakable for a man to share with his drinking buddies, feelings he'd quietly allowed his mama all these years.

Chessor removed every blanket from his mama's bed except a thin sheet to preserve her modesty. The snag in his throat had grown big as an apple, but he swallowed it nevertheless. Without the fire burning in the pot-belly stove, Gracie's cottage was going cold as a mausoleum, and Chessor stood over his mama as she shivered as much as the last bit of energy in her skeletal body would let her.

"You'll be warm soon, Mama," Chessor said. "And then you'll have smoked deer with Daddy until you're full up." Chessor forced himself to look at the woman who'd birthed him, reared him, and switched him so he learned right from wrong. The woman who'd weathered his father's ignorant bullheadedness and drunken foolishness. The woman who'd held her breath until her baby was home from the war, then welcomed him home with the warmth and generosity of a saint. The woman who'd buried her husband before his time, but never begrudged the vices that sent him to the grave early. The woman who, never overbearing, loved Chessor despite his insistence he needed no one, not even her.

Chessor reached across his mama and wrestled her window open. This would be the window she, warm again, would fly out of into her husband's arms. A torrent of frigid air filled Gracie's room, and snow wasted no time collecting on her body.

Chessor kissed his mama on the cheek, and except for the shivering, she was already a corpse. Chessor held the candle in his hand, unable to blow it out, but when the wind whipping snuffed the flame, Chessor told his mama goodbye and set the fat pillar candle back on her vanity.

Chessor opened every window of Gracie's cottage just as she had forty-eight hours before. He struck one of his matches and lit a cigarette inside his mama's house—the first he ever had. He hung it from his lips and stepped outside.

"Life have mercy," Chessor muttered, exhaling a plume of smoke as he started his Jeep. The engine turned over, the wipers beat the snow from the windshield, and the truck's headlamps erupted into the night. Chessor closed his eyes and inhaled long on his smoke. He would return to his mama in the morning, after a night of drinking, a night of numbing. Until then, he could pretend she was still with him.

He jammed the gearshift into first and began his slow descent.

Guy Walks Into a Bar

Milton J. Bates

and orders a beer, a shot of whiskey
or a Bloody Mary. Sometimes he's
a woman, a horse, a duck, a panda,
or a termite. You've heard this story
before, or one just like it, but you
follow it down the familiar road,
watching for an unsuspected turn.

Suppose the guy's a minister: he'll bring
a rabbi and a priest. Otherwise
he'll have to talk to the bartender.
He'll order that drink. He'll ask a question
or be asked. That's how these stories work.

You listen carefully, all ears, because
who wants to be the last to catch
the double meaning, to understand
the misunderstanding, to get the joke?
Who wants to seem as dumb as the guy,
or maybe this time it's the bartender?

You try to memorize the story, word
for word, so you can walk into a bar
and get it right. *Guy walks into a bar,*
you'll say, and everyone will pay attention.
They'll follow you down that road, happy
to be with a guy who knows the way.

NPR Said We Are Made of Stardust

Cindy Veach

Even the pileated woodpecker
        that has been calling from the woods
                that I finally spotted today

high in a dead tree—
        brilliant red crest, black and white
                variegated neck, twice the size

of the red-headed, who is striking
        in its own right, but the pileated
                has the Eldorado of stardust,

the mother lode with that sweeping
        Corinthianesque head, scarlet
                red, regal red—in full command

of the tree he knocks his beak against
        scooping out a nest,
                pitching his voice into the day—

stardust even now shaping him, settling
        on his back and beak as it is
                designing the bugs

he probes for in the belly of the tree.
        As it is designing the sky, the air,
                each first and last breath—

oh industrious, herculean, all knowing
　　　stardust, there should be a church to you,
　　　　　　a temple to you, a mosque to you—

and if the ancient dust of stars is us,
　　　then aren't we the memory of the universe
　　　　　　and this particular pileated woodpecker,

the dinosaur he once was, the elusive dark
　　　matter scientists are searching for,
　　　　　　the sounds they are keening for?

Then aren't we ghosts—our arms, legs
　　　and tongues banging against this rotten tree
　　　　　　carving a place to sleep under the stars.

Promises

Charles Rafferty

I will break
your window to keep
the moon

from staining it.
I will sink
my own armada

to palace you
in driftwood boards.
I will choke

the songs
from a thousand wrens
and stuff them

deep in your pillow.
There is no limit
to the things I'll promise.

Listen. One day
when you notice the dawn
is less

musical and the beach
is written
with broken ships,

prepare
for the moon to enter
your skin,

unimpeded by glass,
to tell you
the darkness is me.

Source

Charles Rafferty

The touch-me-nots tangle
the creek air like a living cloud,
muffling the water already
muted by the hillside
August heat. Sometimes there
is movement, the darting
of small birds. More often
it is anvil-still, humming
with crickets and hidden
frogs. Once, a fox leaped out of it
into broad air and took off
with something in its mouth.
I am afraid to reach beyond
the blossoming crumbs
of aster and phlox. The creek
is in there though.
I hear the gurgle of it
after rain. I see it emerge
far downhill like a boiling
clarity. But here at the top
it gathers like a riddle. Only
the winter can enumerate
the creek-start mysteries—
only the air that kills can show me
the nests and rivulets,
the secret I wanted so badly to hear
that I sweated up a hill
and into its green confusion.

The Universe Revised

Al Maginnes

How many times will I read
the life, the early death
of Keats and wish another end?
Some days it seems a tragedy
so bright and singular
the world never recovered.
Other days it finds its spot
in the ranks of tragedies
that compose the world:
waves dissolve whole coastlines,
bullets find unmeant targets,
planets fail to form among
the gases and dust, the errant
gravities of a universe
too busy to be consistent.
The thunderstorm that whiplashed
through the afternoon tore
another limb from the tree
slowly dying in our front yard.
A scar of yellow wood,
bright as a star, shines raw
where the branch broke
from the tree's body. Every year
a few more limbs, bare
as a skeleton, show through leaves
so pale-green they seem yellow.
Trees were cut flat, fed into
the sulfur-reeking maw
of a paper mill to make this book
about Keats I'm reading now
as though I never read
another, as though this one
might end letting Keats
marry Franny Brawne, write
odes praising the moon-thin
skull of a sleeping son,
live to eighty and die,
his name no longer weighted
with the gravity of a life

→

unfinished. When the tree is gone,
we will notice light falling
where we were used to shade.
Then we won't see it at all.
If we imagine the universe
revised so Keats grows old,
we can page through the drafts
of atoms and small charges,
the depth and grips of matter
that builds on itself and breaks down
to say what will be written
when we step into shadows that will
see us dissolve before they do.

We don't speak of stones or the sea in Western Washington.

We use other words in place of these,
            found out in your poetry.

That's how I knew you weren't from here.

We don't talk the way you do.

Sandra Kleven in Poetry and Prose:
A Review of Defiance Street: Poems and Other Writing

Rob Pockat

"I come to this circus from another country and the words you use sometimes elude me." This first line from the opening poem of Sandra Kleven's outstanding book, *Defiance Street: Poems and other writing*, pushed me back to a time in my life when words and writing were even more of a mystery to me than they are now, a time when the only reading material in my house was the morning news—not the most interesting content for a blossoming reader. Books were the contraband of an unfettered, resistant youth, and when opportunities arose to get my hands on the forbidden fruit of literature, I viewed the spectacle through eyes no different than those of Kleven's subject in that opening poem, "…a little dog, head a-tilt, a-tuned to lively ditties from an old calliope." Beginning with a childlike perspective and concluding with experience that only time and persistence offers, the barker taunts the reader into the tent to view the sideshows, bareback riders, freaks, and clowns. It is, after all, the only show in town.

Sandra Kleven, *Defiance Street: Poems and other writing*, Vered Publishing & Design House, 2013

In *Defiance Street*, Sandra Kleven is a reflective, lyric guide leading readers through realities of love, loss, triumph, and defeat that can only be scripted once passed, the narrative layers thickening and becoming more complex as she explores her own physical, spiritual, and intellectual growth. The complexity, however, is achieved through concision. In the poem "Out of Place in Seattle," for example, she offers readers this image:

We don't speak of stones or the sea in Western Washington.
We use other words in place of these, found out in your poetry.
That's how I knew you weren't from here.
We don't talk the way you do.

The narrator, who is by all accounts in a familiar geographical landscape, considers that place is not only a tangible location but also a familiarity of individual understanding. It is not the subject in this unfamiliar place who talks differently; it is the speaker in her own environment whose perceptions are different. Years have passed and memories have softened, yet time and distance have magnified how perspectives change and how our familiar world develops by attempting to understand it through the views of others.

Our lives are led in the "what if" moments where perceptions of forked roads linger until sentience no longer exists, time's sleight of hand casting an illusive filter on memory. Kleven ends the first section of *Defiance Street* with a short autobiographical essay recalling her days as a twenty-something art model in Seattle and New York, searching for a Holden Caulfieldesque sense of authenticity and partial stasis. Kleven captures this essence by acknowledging that time can and does skew the truth: "Because of deficits in the function of memory and my inclination toward revision, this story is not entirely true, but the important things are, and you should know what to believe by the end." The essay builds upon memory and leaves the reader with an understanding that truth is simply what one believes.

In considering the structure of Kleven's book, I could not help but extend the circus metaphor. Broken into three sections, the text forms three seemingly concentric rings, each containing a separate stage of life. Yet no one ring seems more important than the other at any given time. They are simply vessels that fill our human need to contain and compartmentalize the abstractions of life's events. The second section, "Board Walk to the Gravel Pit," is a collection of poems and reflections on the author's life in Alaska—political in some pieces, introspective in others, and completely heart-rending in others. Yet she skillfully refrains from sentimentality, crafting pieces of art as opposed to simply offering readers a glance into a personal journal.

In life, a human being cannot exist without having at least one horrifically memorable experience. "Open Water," a flash essay about Kleven's life as a behavioral health clinician who worked as a first responder in Alaska, takes the reader into one of her horrifically memorable experiences. These may be two of the most powerful pages I have ever read, and analysis of this piece would not do it justice. While I understand the implications of breaking the rules of subjectivity in reviewing another's work, I can wholeheartedly write that reading *Defiance Street* solely for this piece can only help one grow as a reader, writer, and human being.

There is a progressive growth in the first two sections of the book, an introduction to simple experiences simply written that evolves for both the reader and writer. Kleven's experiences are different from her readers' experiences, to be sure, yet shared universal truths provide symbiosis between author and reader. In the book's third and final section, "Breadfruit, Manna, and Hay," there is an almost logotherapeutic attempt to make meaning of life's sideshows, freaks, and performances—an artistic spiritual exploration, if you will, into how we do, or in some cases don't, manage to carry on. In the section's opening poem, "Saecula Saeculorum," the title itself invokes the philosophy of a world without end. Ours is simply a finite performance of an eternal show. The characters and acts may change, but the tent is always present.

The arts prove spiritually weighty in the final section of *Defiance Street*. "Northwest Reverie," an homage to painter Mark Tobey, is particularly moving to me given my love of abstract expressionism and the fact that Tobey was born in Centerville, a small, one-road town just a few minutes' drive from my home—a place where I often walk the village cemetery to reflect on my own life's meanings and attempt to figure out my place in this larger production. This poem transported me for a moment to Tobey's birthplace, where I've felt the Lake Michigan breeze cool on my summer-warm skin, smelled the pungent odor of a late spring algae bloom, and listened as the waves slapped against the rocky shore of Hika Bay. I am familiar with reverie, and this poem did what great art is meant to do—guide one on his own path to discover meaning.

Defiance Street closes with a finale, the main event—a culmination of performances that crescendo to a thrilling finish. In her essay "The Canny Invention," Kleven draws upon a lifetime of experiences and begins to find her purpose through what one could easily consider a spirit guide. In this final piece, she tells of the guidance she gained from the writings of Theodore Roethke, a perfectly flawed human being who balanced his inner demons with outwardly beautiful poetry. He seems the ideal ringmaster to usher Sandra Kleven, an author, an artist, a virtuoso in her own right, to a place where she can so poignantly share her craft, her art, her show, with audience members who can take a moment to step out of their own lives in order to make sense of them once they step back in.

In a page of final acknowledgements, there is a sentence that reads, "A poet grows in clover, nettles and brine; in puddles, closets, and under covers; in the certain and the maybe." The cover is closed, the circus has ended. The sideshows, bareback riders, freaks, and clowns have packed up, and the caravan has moved on. Yet the images remain, and I sit, a little dog, head a-tilt, a-tuned to ditties from an old calliope. It is, after all, the only show in town.

Suicide Mission

Sandra Kleven

The son of poets Sylvia Plath and Ted Hughes has taken his own life 46 years after his mother gassed herself while he slept. —London Times, March 26, 2009

The Kuskokwim River is frozen in May. Locals buy Kuskokwim Classic lottery tickets guessing the exact hour and minute of break-up—a messy affair, as the broken ice of Western Alaska swishes and tinkles past the town. I didn't buy a ticket in 2008, though one time I came within a day or so of winning.

It still looked like winter in Bethel on that May weekend when my brother Jon called and said he wanted to kill himself. How apt. Suicide is my job. I was carrying the pager for the Native health corporation, on call to evaluate the emotionally impaired, psychotic, and suicidal. By training, I am a licensed clinical social worker. My brother called from Auburn, Washington, two thousand miles away.

The professional decision is an easy one, an application of state law about involuntary commitment. Patients are actively suicidal, or they are not. There are three options: admission to the local hospital; a flight by jet to the psych hospital in Anchorage; or they can go back home. By state statute, they cannot be held unless they are an immediate danger to self or other. We ask, "Do you still want to kill yourself? No? Well, okay then, let's get you out of here!"

Bethel had been my home, off and on, since 1984, most recently working in mental health care. For school and family, I'd relocated to Anchorage, but I was asked to occasionally carry the emergency pager on the weekend. It paid about $650, plus per diem.

Halfway through an MFA degree in poetry, I could jet to Bethel from my home in Anchorage—about four hundred miles, under an hour in flight time. I'd stay at the Longhouse Hotel, and in the (occasionally broken) peace of the weekend, I would do poetry homework.

The pager was clipped at my waist, digging into my gut as I leaned into my laptop. I was editing notes about the poet Muriel Rukeyser. I worked the pager along my waistband to the side, better.

The phone in the room rang. It was about 9:00 p.m. Jon said, "Sam, I am going to kill myself."

I said, "Don't do it, Jon." I worried about the family. I said, "If you do, you will be introducing suicide as the way out in our family. You will be making suicide a family legacy." This was not his day to die. We went on to other subjects, our father's empty house, for one, and talked quite awhile. I didn't follow protocol. But, then, protocol sort of sucks.

My suicide missions started nine years earlier, with two kids from the same village—a boy, about eighteen, and a girl of fourteen. They died by hanging, the girl in December 1998, and the boy just three weeks later, in January 1999. I went to the village funerals for these kids. In the Yup'ik Eskimo culture, bodies remain in the family home for three days while people visit to pay respects. The house is kept cold, as no mortician has injected the syrups of preservation. You can sit on the couch and look on the body, dressed as if for church, surrounded by stuffed animals and other favorite things. Pray or sing. Read their journals. Puzzle out the motivating difficulty. The girl, in her early chaotic teens, wrote—in messy cursive—that she wanted to die because she had eczema. She hanged herself from the top bunk. Her older brother, reading in his bedroom on the other side of the wall, did not hear a thing. Her brother would turn to poetry. I did, too.

Alaska is the suicide capital of America. That particular village lost ten kids to suicide between 1991 and 2001. The dead ranged in age from twelve to twenty. The work makes me feel leaden. Numb and detached. It makes me inexpressibly sad.

There is more trouble in and around Bethel than there should be in a remote town, population 6,200. The problems are mainly due to drinking, even though you can't legally buy booze in Bethel. You can ship in drink for personal use, but those who can't wait get it from bootleggers, buying the commercial product for as much as $100 a fifth.

Those desperate for drink will steal anything with alcohol content. Listerine and Aqua Velva are locked behind glass in the grocery stores. People have died drinking antifreeze, thinking it might relieve the shakes, the desperate urge. Drunk people, young and old, die from aspirating vomit, alcohol poisoning, violence, suicide, driving when drunk, death by drowning in summer and by freezing in winter.

Families, trying to function around drink, end up angry, heartsick or bitter—and, when one more dies, the survivors try to get by, but it gets old and resilience fails. Faith in good gets shaky. Troubles bring cops and child protection workers. Children end up in foster care, not sure what is happening, crying for their parents and begging to go home.

Bethel is the service hub for fifty-two villages spread over a region about the size of Oregon state. This accounts for another 20,000 people, most Yup'ik or Athabascan. There are a few trails between villages but no real roads, and the distances from outpost to outpost can be hundreds of miles. In some villages, people commit suicide in numbers as high as thirty times the national average.

One night, I had to get four suicidal people into Bethel, by plane or boat. After I worked this out, I got another call. A woman was feeling depressed. The call was patched through from the hospital. I asked the caller, "Do you feel like hurting yourself?"

She said, "No." I found myself thinking, *Why not? Everybody else is!*

Some have been seen in the ER trying to overdose on Tylenol. They are treated with activated charcoal, black goop, mouth smeared like a baby eating mud. It's intended to absorb the drug. Many are brought in with superficial cutting—new marks that join a track of scars laddering the arm—evidence that they have been doing it for years. I have seen eyes that seem to bleed, blood vessels of the whites having burst as a result of hanging and barely surviving—because the rope broke or because someone heard something that didn't sound right, cut them down and got them breathing.

Or screechy drunks raging, "I want to die!" who, believably, do not remember a thing when they sober up. Few, as a rule, share the anguish of the friends and family members sitting with them in the ER. The patients are calm, glib and, if emotional at all, mad about being detained. They promise they won't do it again, and most of the time they don't, as if the dramatic gesture filled the need.

As a small boy growing up in Seattle, Jon was afraid of dogs. I was older and I looked out for him. He was sensitive to things.

When he was three, we'd ride in the beige backseat of the family's maroon Plymouth. Stopping for gas, a guy would come to the window: "What can I getcha?"

Dad would hand him a buck. "A dollar's worth of regular." While gas flowed, the guy would squirt cleaner on our windows and wipe them with a paper towel. That dollar went a long way.

We were always driving the five-mile route between two sets of grandparents. It ran along the railroad tracks, passing a wrecking yard. The heaped catastrophe of crashed cars devastated Jonny. His lower lip trembled. His eyes filled and spilled as he mouthed, "Bwoke cars, bwoke cars." I thought it was cute and funny, but hid my smile and said, "Don't cry, Jonny. It's okay. They are going to car heaven."

Mom and Dad had four more kids. I was Big Sister Caretaker. When Jon was about eight, Mom moved out, taking all us kids with her. That year, Jon flunked third grade. I was less destroyed by our parents' split, though more angry and defiant.

When Jon was about eleven, Mom came after me with a badminton racket, angry about my backtalk. She turned it on edge, hitting me anywhere she could. Jon watched in anxious protest. "Don't hurt Sandy, Mom. Please don't hurt Sandy."

As an adult, Jon followed Seattle's Seahawks. After a big play on TV, he'd leap to his feet shouting, pointing at the screen. "Did you see that, Sam? Did you see that?"

Jon married three times, divorced. He became a licensed pilot. He got a BA degree. He was a baby-rocker at a hospital—a volunteer comforting the babies born to addicts. He was an Air Force Reserve Medic and worked at Boeing for decades and could soon retire.

But he never got over his daughter's death. In 1995, when she was twenty-two, his only child died in a motorcycle accident. She was in the army, having joined the military at his urging. Her medals, trophies, and folded flag presented by the honor guard crowded a glass cabinet in Jon's living room. Jon struggled with anxiety and depression. He gave up flying. Worked with a psychiatrist. Took Zyprexia.

With money from his daughter's military life insurance, Jon bought a doublewide mobile home set in a well-kept Auburn, Washington trailer park. My oldest son, an adult, lived with him, as did Jon's grown stepson. They were three guys, camping out together. They spent a lot of time with our dad in Seattle's Fremont neighborhood, where Dad had returned to the house where he grew up.

Dad died at eighty, just after Thanksgiving in 2007.

When Jon called me in Bethel, about six months had passed since Dad's death. Jon was sixty then. Dad appointed his youngest son, Dennis, as estate executor, but after Dad's death, Jon talked Dennis into letting him take over. This was a step down the wrong road for Jon.

We all needed money so we decided to sell Dad's house—even though it had been in the family since 1927. This little bungalow in Fremont was now worth half a million. No one could afford to buy it. No one really wanted to live there.

I wrote a poem about Dad's house, about our failure letting it go after eighty years in the family. I wrote, "Where hands touched hands across six generations, on our sad watch the weakest link has broken." I read it to Jon the night he called me in Bethel. I think about that sometimes. It was a little harsh.

Six weeks after that call, the link broke. Jon hanged himself in his mobile home. His stepson found him. My son arrived as the paramedics rolled him out.

After Jon died, our family behaved badly. Previously nice people accused others of driving my brother to suicide. Some thought they knew what Jon was thinking and why he did it. Those who probably knew the least, those with less stake, became the most vocal—venting online, writing accusations like, "It's your fault, you greedy bitch."

We took sides. The older siblings rolled their eyes at angry screeds from the families of the younger ones. Our youngest sisters were born after mother remarried. Because they have a different father, they weren't closely involved in issues of Dad's estate. Married and with kids of their own, this group was angry and spoke their mind openly, on listservs, where others could read. MySpace posts carried other mean messages. They were aimed mainly at me, the oldest; the one who lived furthest away. As the parent figure in this ever-growing family group, they probably thought I should have saved Jon. Maybe I could have.

The recriminations astounded me more than they hurt me. Ten years in suicide work had not prepared me for this distorted discharge of pain. I would have expected softly lit rooms; voices of compassion saying things like "Don't blame yourself. He had been so unhappy for so long. Never the same, really, since he lost Kary."

On the Internet, some nieces jumped to my defense. My own kids wanted me to weigh in and say something to defend myself, but I stuck with my mom's early teaching: ignore it. Rise above it. Fighting the distraction caused by this background drama, we worked on arrangements, wrote Jon's obituary, choose the site of the grave, made decisions about the service.

We buried Jon next to his daughter in Bellingham, Washington's Bayview Cemetery. Later, the family settled into workable ways of functioning. Some avoiding others, the Alaska contingent able to fully retreat. Those who were angry never knew that Jon called me in Bethel or that I read him a poem that accused him of failure—if he took it that way. There were reasons to target me—I could have done more. But they didn't know this.

I wonder about the poem; if the poetic act of attention might generate a spill-over effect that could make things better. *She nailed it there. Let's grieve it, together.* I remember something of that feeling, that I was telling a truth that might be cleansing—as it was painful.

About my warning? I don't know if he was concerned about creating a family suicide legacy, but I don't think he knew what a mess he would make.

What Jon did with rope and the weight of his body was not like one who steps off a chair and dangles helplessly to die, suspended. It was more like those who choke themselves to intensify a sexual climax. The stricture used was looped over the bathroom doorknob, his weight given over to it when he lowered himself to the floor. He could have stopped the choking up to the point where he passed out. He left a note, and this serves as confirmation that it was a planned suicide and not an accident related to kinky sexual games. He wrote that his personal life was "swirling out of control." He wrote that the sale of the house was his last hope.

After his death, Jon's cell phone held a voicemail message from Dad's lawyer. In a needling voice, harsh to the ear, the lawyer said that the sale, thought to be imminent, was not going through. Jon may well have heard that as a final message—death to his last hope. The sale was not delayed. It closed on the day of Jon's funeral.

Even though the house sold for $498,000, our dad had taken a loan on it of about $100,000. Our disabled cousin owned a quarter share of the house. There were debts to pay, and when it settled, less than $100,000 was shared among Dad's seven children.

Alaska was my refuge. I could leave it all behind, and I gladly boarded the plane for the North.

Next, for me, came the winter of Fairbanks. I flew to small villages to teach preschoolers how to play nicely. No more trips to Bethel. No more pager alarms to trigger my secondary PTSD.

Twenty times in the winter after Jon's death, I flew to Fairbanks. From there, I'd catch a smaller plane and fly toward the dark icescape of the upper Yukon—to places with names like Allakaket, Tanana, and Kaltag. These trips lasted just a day or two. One time, in the Fairbanks airport, I listened to Alaska's Sarah Palin debating Joe Biden. I was in Allakaket, sleeping on a couple of beanbag chairs and periodically checking election returns on CNN.com when I cheered Obama's victory.

At the same time, I worked my way through the MFA program, reading the poets of the 1960s and '70s—Lowell, Sexton, Plath, and Kumin, reading collections, journals, letters, and biographies. I read about Plath's suicide.

Sylvia killed herself on February 11, 1963. In Sylvia's poems, I met her son, Nicholas Hughes: "You are the one / Solid the spaces lean on, envious / You are the baby in the barn."

I was a high school senior in 1963. On the Monday before Plath's death, I was kicked out of school for "getting myself pregnant." I was turned out to walk home that day, as if I had something catchy.

The year before I got pregnant, I had made a suicide gesture myself. Maybe gesture isn't the right word. A gesture would be subtler. This was a suicide *attempt*. I swallowed pills, but I had been tentative. I did not swallow a lethal handful of pills, but instead, took just one pill from every bottle in the pharmacy above the refrigerator. There were twenty plus bottles of prescription medicines, some current, the rest stockpiled through neglect. I swallowed the meds, even vitamins, and self-consciously topped them off with a swig of whiskey from my parents' commemorative Space Needle decanter. I was upset about my mother, who slapped me, belittled my feelings, put me down, and yet, left me in charge of all the kids (four sisters under five) with orders to clean up all their messes. I was the oldest, the caretaker and housekeeper. The three others, who spanned the years between the little girls and me, including my brother, Jon, moved in with Dad when Mom remarried in 1959.

After I took the pills, I lay down to die, but felt like a phony, as if I had not earned this private drama. I had threatened a few times to kill myself—screaming at my mother, "I want to die. I hate you. I don't want to live anymore." Mother would say, "Go ahead. Can I get you a knife?" Psyching me out—I knew it. A tactic. Fairly effective since the only way to prove her wrong was to die. Even then, I saw this as no way to win the point.

In order to appear *sincerely* suicidal (not a phony), I didn't tell anyone or let myself be discovered—with this exception: I got up from the floor and walked three miles to my best friend's house. I told her what I had done. Neither of us were properly alarmed. I was much like those I would later evaluate—nonchalant. I would have gotten furiously angry if I were taken somewhere. I *did* want to be discovered, but it had to be by chance so my pain would be seen as real, not contrived. Then, all would surround me with tears, caresses and alarm. My friend kept my secret and we got through the day, only halfway remembering to keep an eye out for any unexpected dying.

The only difference between what I had done and a completed suicide was in the mix of medicines. By taking one of each pill, I was creating a pharmaceutical Russian roulette. I *could* have concocted a lethal mix. If I had died, the results would have resonated through my family for decades, possibly, for generations. I lived and left no ripple.

Did Jon expect to be found while he could still be saved? Like me, did he try to make a "serious enough" gesture to show others how bad things were? If we caught him and saved him, did he hope that we would stop pushing him about Dad's estate, stop asking him for accountability? As noted, Jon hanged himself from the bathroom doorknob while seated on the floor. According to the medical examiner, it was like going to sleep. The autopsy showed no drugs or alcohol.

According to some writers, there are indications that Sylvia Plath expected to be saved. There were regular visitors who might have arrived in time. Was she hoping only to send the message—this is how much I hurt? Her children, Nicholas and his sister, Frieda, very young children, were sleeping in their room. Sylvia blocked their door with towels to protect them from the gas.

How exactly do you put your head in an oven? Don't you have to rest your head on something? The oven rack? When you pass out, won't you fall to the floor and, by default, get a whiff of better air? Or is this the sort of gas that creeps deadly around the ankles, more fatal near the floor? How do you die with your head in an oven? How do you hang yourself from a door knob? Were they surprised to find themselves dead?

After Plath died, Ted Hughes wrote that his infant son's eyes "became wet jewels, / The hardest substance of the purest pain / As I fed him in his high white chair." I ache when I read that. I could see that child, Nicholas Hughes, betrayed at age two.

During my Fairbanks winter, while waiting at the airport and while flying, I read more on Plath, Ted Hughes, his next wife, the other deaths. I read Plath's unabridged journal and noted that she sounded shallow, all intensity, self, and boys. I was much the same in high school, twelve years younger, but also coming out of the 1950s, with a Prince Charming orientation, always looking for a cuter boy.

I had no idea that *Nicholas* of Plath's biography lived in Alaska, that he lived in Fairbanks and had been a professor at the central branch of my own MFA college. I knew none of this until I read the news report of Nicholas Hughes' death in March 2009: "Nicholas Hughes hanged himself at his home in Alaska after battling against depression for some time.... He was 47, unmarried with no children of his own and had until recently been a professor of fisheries and ocean sciences at the University of Alaska Fairbanks."

Six months had passed since Jon's death. I'd been working on poems about it and, as part of my coursework, absorbing the life of Plath and Hughes, the children. My first coherent poem on the subject of Jon's suicide was accepted for publication by a journal—as luck would have it, I thought, with some bitterness. As I worked on poetry and suicide, Plath's grown son had lived close by, in that remote, unlikely, station, far from the London of his birth. Now, he too was dead.

Nicholas Hughes left no chance of rescue. He hanged himself, alone, in a shed. His girlfriend, who now lives with what's left, found his body. Some reports mentioned recent disagreements about his father's estate, but Ted Hughes died more than ten years earlier so it is hard to imagine these issues spiking to a new pitch. Someone wrote that he missed his dad. Jon missed our dad, too.

In the death notices, I read that Nicholas Hughes resigned from his position at the college in order to devote more time to his pottery—not poetry—pottery. He did not connect with the literary world at all. He was a scientist and a potter. There was no connection to his mother's death, they write. News stories after Nicholas Hughes' death mention that he was inclined toward depression. He had never married. He leaves no children.

His sister Frieda Hughes described him as *a loving brother, a loyal friend to those who knew him and, despite the vagaries that life threw at him,* he maintained an almost childlike innocence and enthusiasm for the next project or plan.

Chris Green, a London journalist, wrote, "Some people cope with terrible suffering while others succumb.... People learn coping behavior from their families and from those around them. If someone close to them chooses suicide then it may seem like an option for them, too. It raises the idea that, when the pressure grows, this is what people do."

Did Sylvia Plath's suicide kill Nicholas? Was a thread or fuse put in place then, to burn through the life of a family, until a day perfect with things terrible? Does this precisely wrong day set in motion the final sequence of a slow suicide machine? Can something set up decades ago lurch into action, so that a ball drops, and a person says, "Today, I end it," drawing a noose against the neck so that life goes out in a silent catastrophe of sleep? Did Plath's act offer suicide as an option, saying, in a sense, "in our family, this is what is done?"

In the Fairbanks airport, I drank beer and started this poem. Later, I found the quotes, knew I would use "the baby in the barn," for sure.

Orestes

Sylvia your son has done.
Has done. Has done.
A son undone.

A plumb bob. A fell swoop.
A fraying fuse
Your son gone out.

    The family shoe, *Undo, undo.*
    Short letters rant, *Do not, Do not.*
    A roaring score, *Alors, alors.*
    The worst is true.
    You pay on blue.

Two, of course, there are two.
It seems perfectly natural now ———

The down dog tree, whose branches clamp
    your total lack, in fact, they rip
    the cage of your lost rib in two.
A man unstrung in black out back,
    whose knees play timpani, Constant C
    against the oven door B flat.

Sweet in his hospital icebox.
A simple frill at the neck.

Then you come around
    with your frown in your hand
    like a blemish of fish,
    like a Flemish witch, a twitch
    to the cuttlefish agony, you do not face
    until this death wishing sore unwell

→

> meets you in your cookery
> to rhyme a rank reunion song.
>
> Eyes run with ruddy scrim.
> Sylvia, you remember him;
> the baby in the barn
> cut down.

I felt immediately ashamed. The poem was ruthless, cruel, ghastly—the image of the eyes, borrowed from those I had seen in those nearly dead from hanging. I was mocking Plath's style, too. How did I dare attack this darling of the lost and lonely? I worried about entering the poem into the world, but did. It was published, and a note I received from the editor helped me feel it was understood and sanctioned beyond my interior outburst of accusation. Poor Sylvia. Suicide and blame. I was doing it, too, just like they did to me.

Because I am a suicide specialist, trained in suicide doctrine, I believe the only one to blame for a suicide is the one who takes hand against self. Certain circumstances could change this, but only to a degree. Someone might be "driven to suicide" in a prisoner of war camp and in other serious situations. A late-stage terminal illness might make suicide a rational choice, with the death being in a sense the fault of the illness. The task after a suicide is to comfort the living and to console those who torture themselves with blame.

Jon was not a prisoner of war. One central problem was the fact that Jon was carrying seven "payday" loans. You see this kind of lender in a strip mall, most of them national chains, bright signage, located among cable companies and coffee shops. They offer to advance money against a future paycheck. Every payday, Jon paid back seven loans. Then, he borrowed the same amount again to have money to live on and pay other bills. As he did this, he felt like he was getting away with something illegal, putting something over on these companies that would get him in trouble if he were caught.

After he was dead, I saw confirmation of his payday loans in his checkbook. Duplicates of cashed checks showed that he paid back the loans, about $5600, every pay period. Considering just the time involved in repeating these transactions every month and then adding the despair of the trap and the sense that he was the criminal, it's easy to imagine the grinding slippage toward futility. There is more. He gambled at the nearby casino. I don't know the whole story. He saw selling Dad's house as the solution. That was clear at the end.

But Jon wasn't thinking straight in the months before his death. He'd see pending catastrophe in letters about renewing car insurance. I'd have him scan the papers and email them to me. I could explain away his misreading and misperceptions, soothing his panic. I hear that echo from our childhood: "It's okay, Jonny."

The poem about the house was too much to share with a brother thinking suicide. But it was a poem and it was new and it captured the troubles, so I read it to him when he called me in Bethel. I have held a vain hope about it, but mostly feel my folly.

> We let this house slip sad away
> Like children play at real estate
> whose dad will lunchbox home at six,

→

and pull down all the signs we made.

Not like it was when we were small
to pluck and clutch at grandma's skirt
to hide within her irises
and watch the family break and fall,
loose change from a blue Vicks jar

Until we saw what they had done
we did not think it possible.
If their love could turn like milk
what would they do with six loud kids?
Vacant gaze turns evidence,
an empty house, a family gone.

Nickel rolls slapped 'cross our palms
before the long good-bye was spoken.
Where hand touched hand across six generations
on our sad watch the weakest link has broken.

All of this in the poem: the embrace of our grandmother, the divorce that shattered our world, the splitting of the children—I never cried about it, not then, not now. It's flatlined, dead and gone. A sickness that turned everyone sour. So much, so sad, unsaid.

Maybe my sloppy interventions in May held him until July 15. Would it have been better if I sent the police to his house that night for the standard "welfare check"? How would that help? Jon to the ER, checked by someone like me. "So, do you want to kill yourself? No? Well, maybe your nephew can keep an eye on you at home. No reason to keep you." That's a pretty succinct summary, if you add to it hours of waiting alone in an exam room.

The weakest link broke. It hurts to live, and yet most choose to live until called by the final authorities, those laws of physics and biology that take us out. A long life can bring one to bedsides of both birth and death. To a witness, birth struggles more terribly. But there is apparent reward in both becoming and unbecoming: arrival and release. Most people wait for the final fight—prepared to rage against light's decline and fall. Jon brought it on. Even with his troubles, he leaves me in the dark.

Sometimes my judgment is faulty. Everybody is guilty of some foolish act. I have tried to hurt myself in order to hurt someone else. Hurt someone else wanting to wake them up. One thing leads to another. When any of my four grown sons tells me they are feeling down, dimmed by whatever reversals accumulate around a life, I am quick to ask, "Do you feel like hurting yourself?" My mind runs the trail of loss, sees unremitting anguish. "You're okay? All right. Good. You're sure?" Don't do it. Don't do it. Suicide ruins everything. I had to write a warning. Is this what you want to be known for?

For Jon, Once My Brother

This end stains a whole life.
This end sets loose a tide to seep through the frames   →

that hold days distinct
coloring all that came before the knots
and coils of your most difficult hour.

Sixty years crossed off, the day, I'll say it—
You choked yourself to death.
And ink ran from the corners of your mouth
until there was nothing to hang but a load of darks
dripping whispers. *He killed himself, you know.*

Struck by this: that Jon's years rocking drug babies, his proud time in the US Air Force, and, later, as a veteran's advisor in a college (he guided me into college at twenty-nine, a veteran mother, shy about taking classes)—that all of this vanished and he is remembered, first, as one who died by his own hand. Like Sylvia Plath, whose legacy became a path, a gesture, an invitation. Take this way out. So many suicides are referenced as having followed her, in imitation and, apparently, admiration. And, then, in a dark shed in remote Alaska, Nick jumped over the candlestick.

But, I would wish to erase my brother's suicide legacy, Sylvia's too, with a no-suicide pact, calling my family, my sons, calling the reader, calling my emergency room patients to join it. Survive along with me. Let us advertise our belonging, our kinship. Let us live on an island of life, bright with reconciliation and promises honored. I will be so faithful, if you promise this prize. I would live with a terminal disease, vicious bites of fate, with guilt and loss. I will try to live, even, with terror. I will ride my horsey life to an end that comes from outside causes. I will do it, if you will. I cannot live with your suicide. It is too cruel. Too final. Too filled with dreadful and unanticipated consequence.

In Bethel, when the Kuskokwim breaks up, the change is immediate: Two, three days watching the ice flow by, rumors of ice jams upriver. Brief flooding, if the ice piles up downstream, more fun than anything, "Wow. Cool." Water creeps up over the road. When you see foam on the river, like clumps of dirty suds, the ice is gone, herring are in the river, and open skiffs take off hoping to catch them by the dozen. Soon the salmon will be running.

A New Model for Workplace Advancement

Rich Ives

I was promised I could have the words I needed
but the controllers gave me no words.
I found other words arrogant in the street.
They demanded I pick them up.

I kept searching. I found quiet words.
They offered me a way to go home,
but I had no home. Home was only
a way to rest when I was sleeping.

The children had weapons,
and they used them to row across
when the river got too busy ignoring them.
They used them when they had
nowhere to go.

Come this way, said the street words.
Come this way, said the quiet words.
So I let them fall from both sides of my mouth.

Finally, the children learn to operate their weapons quietly.
We called them successful to see if that would make them play.
We gave them medical terms like *cry* and *laughter*.
They used them when they had
nowhere to go.

The children had discovered that having
nowhere to go required no weapons
and was more dangerous.

Soon the children were old, and the words they needed
were looking for them everywhere, which was older.
I live there now with the lost children. I do not appear
to have forgotten anything.

Francisca

Peter Schaller

Descanso

Peter Schaller

Soul's Parable

Michael Collins

This is not the breeze that held the twelve villagers together. Or the crows who squawked, guarding the forest to the west. Those gathered are not standing in a circle. There is no hawk on the horizon, no woman with subtle wrinkles below her eyes with her hair in a bun who will not submit to tears, nor any such thing as a small girl delighting a haze of rose petals around the couple in the center. This is not the small bag packed and waiting behind the table at his mother's, but only the ring he slipped around the finger of the last girl he would kiss. It was springtime. The year that the war came.

3 a.m. Thinking—Misquamicutt Beach, Rhode Island

Eugene Goldin

Won't the ocean ever stop relentlessly pounding the shore?
And, why does the shore accept this arrangement and timelessly?
It's getting uncomfortably obvious that they can't seem to
pull themselves away from each other.
While squirming within this belief, I simply can't turn away—and give them their privacy.
Could it be that the ocean loves pounding away while the
shore loves being pounded?
Additionally, if the ocean was to stop, would the shore begin to doubt
the relationship?
Might the shore, then, suspect an affair with a different element was
in the works?
If the shore was to pick up its possessions and leave, what would the
ocean do with itself?
Could it find a different partner or a hobby?
And anyway, where would the shore go?
Perhaps, each would de- and re-materialize—
joining alternate realms?
And if this was to occur, what then would become of these questions?

Rest

Joseph Briggs

Cat

Müesser Yeniay

In the evening
at a cold bus stop
a huge cat
inside darkness
drank my whole love

I am his fur
I hugged, I did not give up

the clouds were divided
as if they would suffice to earth

his roof was of his ears
his house was of his paws

his concern and joy
was the place of the world
where nobody lived

and there
I embraced him
with all my arms

(Translation from Turkish by the poet)

Some Kind of Holiness

Robert Vivian

Then I didn't go back, and I never returned. And I was never the same, not even the way I looked at sunlight lofting through the tree or heard birds singing of the seasons and their own hymns of flying. And I told the air, I told the earth, I told the sky I couldn't do it anymore and oh, how they understood, oh, how they cherished the surrender and the awakening that was like coming to water for the first time—and then I started to look for materials to build my own wings and flight became a living, wide-awake dream bent on destiny and it was not far-fetched, not impossible but something just out of reach that I was getting ever closer to and then I saw the earth as an acorn in a little girl's hand proffered shyly for my consideration, and then I was delight, I was laughter, I was sexual surprise, I was streaming, I was sunshine, I was rain, I was treetop, I was color-bursting flower and petals floppy and wet with dew, and I was another bird singing and another bird racing through the air with wings flashing like rainbow, and then I couldn't not whisper paradise, I couldn't not say lovely and uppermost, couldn't not say beautiful fish, and I didn't go back and I wouldn't go back because the holiness had claimed me, even if they tried to drag me back and then I could breathe and I knew I would never return, that I would never go back to that place and then I could no longer taste bitterness though I could taste sorrow and then I went to the heart of nectar in a warm chemical bath and I said Rise to the river and the river rose as if to wash over me and then all around was a shining light that almost burned off my eyebrows and then I was grape, I was wine, and then the waving grass sang to me and I opened my hands and they were wet with tears and then I felt seizures of electricity deep within and I knew weather was ancient and wise and always and then I asked to take the torch and knew myself as fire, as immolation and sacrifice, as some kind of holiness, talisman of blessing and choir of many moons and many summers, and then a stranger took my hand and kissed it, and then I got down on my knees at the mouth of a river and then I stroked the fur of the wild dog who suddenly appeared before me and his fur gave off blue sparks and magic and then I tried to howl at the stars and then the voice of God spoke to me and said Be patient, Be gentle and then I read the poems deep inside the grooves of bark and then I started sucking on a pebble to stave off desert thirst and the madcap speeches starting to claim me in gusts of headlong praise and then a single falling leaf held me in rapt beholding and a great light broke over my head in halo and then I memorized the prayer that does not end and always begin with Dear Creator Spirit and then I was notebook spiraling out of control and I knew raiment, I knew the secrets of color and I couldn't go back anymore to that other place wracked with doubt and fear though traces of it remained in the smell of burnt rubber and then freedom crowned me with a sycamore branch and all I could say was Star, star, beautiful star, and then I reached out to you, I reached out to everyone, and then I said Love and I said Poem and I said Forgive me and I said Unspeakable beauty and then I said Thy will be done and I said My, what a beautiful cake and I said Thou movest me and I said Let's dance on the bar and I said I'm hard from all this wanting and I said I once held a fish and it was like holding the whole world and I was, I was and I said Take my hand and I said Take my arm and then I knew what heaven was, what it really is, and I knew I didn't have to be afraid of men with guns and official stamps and then I knew I was almost free, that I was almost ready for nuptials, that my life, any life was an astonishing occurrence that would not end but morph into a different set of colors, and then I said as clearly and evenly as it was in me to speak, I can't go back and I won't go back and this is the writ and the proof of it for even my blood has changed back to the shining ink of stars: and so Father, Mother, brother, sister and all the dearly departed, you don't have to hold the door for me. See, I have already sailed right on through like a sudden breeze light as breathing after much labor and struggle in the rest that comes at end of day and the glass of red wine standing on the table as if it wants to whisper something very holy and very private and very, very simple, something like peace.

Blue

Sally Houtman

Lately I am noticing an unspoken
understanding between things—

a quiet order in the way the rope neither
welcomes the knot nor scorns the burn,

and the sky does not beg the ocean
to give it back its blue.

Innuendos

Danny Earl Simmons

The way the steeple juts
from the church top
like somebody's zealous
overcompensation.

The way the woodstove creaks
in expansion as the fire builds inside;
the way it readies itself for stoking
and the lingering afterglow.

The way the wind presses
its finger to the lips of a dandelion bloom
just before hushing it into gentle spasms
of letting everything go.

If This Poem Were a Book

Kaz Sussman

If this poem were a book
on the cover would be a photo
of the author, much younger
with his daughter, content
in his arms. Inside,

the pages would be supple
as her smile, back
before she discovered
I was not a god and her
self, but a minor deity.

It would be dedicated to the one
who will never find the time
to assess its weight, always
too busy these days, reading
the fiction of strangers.

If this poem were a book
I would keep it near
the woodstove, on the mantle
with the matches, ready

to be used to start the fire
if by coincidence it's cold
on the day she comes
to clean out the house.

We're Sorry

Lee Kisling

For horseshoes press 1, for hand grenades press 2
Please spell the name of the person whose name you are spelling
Please hang your clothes on the line
We're sorry, the number you have dialed is your own number
We're sorry, we can't come to the phone any more.

If you would like to hear more apologies press 9 now
We're sorry, did you say *Iztaccihuatl?*
We're really very very sorry.

For denial press 6, for anger press 7, for bargaining press 8, for depression press 9,
        for acceptance press 1
For despair press 2, for dementia press 3
For an apology in Spanish press 5
If you are also sorry press 6
We're sorry, did you say *stabbed?*

If you have a Chinese phone select the button that looks like a crooked house
        with a bird on the roof
Please hang up, check the number and try again (after picking up, of course)
For Q press pound, for pound press Q, for Ezra Pound press Q pound
We're sorry, please stay on the ledge and Shorty will be with you
For a press pass prease press 7
We sorry, he not work here. He gone.

For confession press 1, for penance press 2, for extreme unction press 3, for Room
        Service press 4
If you are an astronomer press star
If you are reporting a lost dog press pound
If you are an astronomer reporting a lost dog press star pound

If you can't find your car
If you wish you could start over as a child
If you married the wrong person and your heart is frozen
We're sorry, your call is not very important to us
No one will be with you shortly
Please stay on the line.

Contributor Notes

MICHAEL ALBRIGHT has published poems in various journals and periodicals, including *Pembroke Magazine, Blast Furnace, Boston Literary Magazine, Indefinite Space, Inflectionist Review, Uppagus, U.S. 1 Worksheets, The New People, Pittsburgh Post-Gazette*, and others. Michael lives on a windy hilltop near Greensburg, Pennsylvania with his wife, Lori, and an ever-changing array of children and other animals.

JENNIFER AUDETTE lives in Vermont. She gets paid to play with soil, plants and produce at Walker Farm. Her stories have appeared in *Fiction Fix* and *Crack the Spine*, and she's grateful for the folks at The Writer's Center in White River Junction, Vermont who help her develop as a writer. If you find feathers, rocks or skeletal remains (non-human, sicko!) that you'd like to donate to her collection, please contact her: jennifer1million@gmail.com.

Poet PAUL SCOT AUGUST is originally from Chicago but has spent the second half of his life in Wisconsin. He has an MA in Creative Writing from UW-Milwaukee. He is a former poetry editor of *Cream City Review* and has been nominated three times for a Pushcart Prize. His poetry has appeared in *Mead: the Magazine of Literature & Libations, Lindenwood Review, Louisville Review, South Dakota Review, Tygerburning, Connotation-Press, Midwestern Gothic, Los Angeles Review, Dunes Review, Naugatuck River Review, Passages North*, and elsewhere. He currently lives in the Milwaukee area with his two children.

MILTON J. BATES retired from teaching at Marquette University and moved to Marquette, Michigan. His nonfiction books include, most recently, *The Bark River Chronicles: Stories from a Wisconsin Watershed* (Wisconsin Historical Society Press, 2012). His poems have appeared or are forthcoming in *Great Lakes Review, Midwestern Gothic, O-Dark-Thirty, Peninsula Poets*, and *The Wallace Stevens Journal*.

B.J. BEST is the author of three books of poetry: *But Our Princess Is in Another Castle* (Rose Metal Press, 2013), *Birds of Wisconsin* (New Rivers Press, 2010), and *State Sonnets* (sunnyoutside, 2009). *I got off the train at Ash Lake*, a verse novella, is forthcoming from sunnyoutside in 2014.

DOUG BOLLING's poetry has appeared widely in literary journals, including *Comstock Review, Tribeca Poetry Review, Blue Unicorn, Water~Stone Review, Fox Cry Review, Wallace Stevens Journal, English Journal*, and *Bluestem*, and he was recently interviewed by *The Missing Slate* for the Poet of the Month feature. He has received five Pushcart nominations, has graduate degrees from Iowa, and currently lives in Flossmoor, Illinois, part of the greater Chicago area.

JOSEPH BRIGGS is a poet, photographer, and truck driver living in Madison, Wisconsin. His photography can be seen in a number of journals, including *Prick of the Spindle, Subliminal Interiors, Weave Magazine*, and *Hothouse Magazine*.

SUSAN CARR graduated from The School of The Museum of Fine Arts, Boston/Tufts in 2003 with an MFA. She is currently represented by Giampietro Gallery in New Haven, Connecticut. Susan tells stories in pictures using the tools of photography, paint, and video.

THOMAS COCHRAN was raised in Haynesville, Louisiana. His work includes the novels *Roughnecks* (Harcourt, 1999) and *Running the Dogs* (Farrar, Straus & Giroux, 2007). Nonfiction and poetry have appeared under his name in *Oxford American, Rattle, Gray's Sporting Journal*, and other publications. He lives with his wife in rural northwest Arkansas.

MICHAEL COLLINS is a graduate of Kalamazoo College, the Warren Wilson College MFA Program for Writers, and Drew University. He teaches creative and expository writing at New York University. His work has recently appeared or will appear in *BlazeVOX, Dressing Room Poetry Journal, Red Savina Review, Blood Lotus Journal, Mobius, Grist, Kenning Journal, Pank, Smartish Pace*, and *SOFTBLOW*. He lives in Mamaroneck, New York, with his wife, Carol.

GREGORY CROSBY is a recovering art critic and journalist. His poetry has appeared in several publications, including *Court Green, Epiphany, Copper Nickel, Leveler, Ping Pong, Rattle, Sink Review, Jacket, Pearl*, and *The Minetta Review*. He teaches creative writing at Lehman College in The Bronx.

MICHELLE DONAHUE hails from Southern California but currently lives in the cold, cold land of Iowa. She is an MFA candidate in Creative Writing and Environment at Iowa State, where she is the managing editor of *Flyway*. Her work has been published in *Whiskey Island, Redactions, Front Porch Journal*, and others. You can find her online at http://michelledonahue1.wordpress.com.

CHARLES FINN is the editor of *High Desert Journal*, a literary and fine arts magazine out of Missoula, Montana, and author of *Wild Delicate Seconds: 29 Wildlife Encounters* (Oregon State University Press, 2012). His essays and poetry have appeared in a wide variety of literary journals, anthologies, newspapers, and consumer magazines, including *The Sun, Northern Lights, Wild Earth, Silk Road, Open Spaces, Whitefish Review, High Country News, Writers on the Range*, and many others. Originally from Vermont, he lives in Missoula with his wife, Joyce Mphande-Finn, and their two cats, Pushkin and Lutsa.

GENE GOLDFARB, who lives on Long Island, has resumed writing after working as a judge for over thirty years. His poems recently appeared in *Cliterature, Empty Sink, River & South Review, Annapurna*, and *Livid Squid*. Additional poems are scheduled to appear in *Lalitamba, A Narrow Fellow, SLANT, Thin Air*, and *Stray Branch*.

EUGENE GOLDIN was born in Manhattan and raised in Queens, New York. He teaches at Long Island University, maintains an active yoga practice, and enjoys a glass of good wine. His most recent poetry has appeared in *The Artistic Muse* and *eleven to seven literary art magazine*.

JOHN GREY is an Australian-born poet. His writing has been published in *International Poetry Review, Vallum*, and the science fiction anthology *The Kennedy Curse*. Work is forthcoming in *Bryant Literary Magazine, Natural Bridge*, and *Oyez Review*.

Originally from the flatlands of central Illinois, JUSTIN HAMM now lives near Twain territory in Missouri. He is the founding editor of *the museum of americana* and the author of the chapbooks *Illinois, My Apologies* (RockSaw Press, 2011) and *The Everyday Parade / Alone With Turntable, Old Records* (Crisis Chronicles Press, 2013). His work has appeared in *Nimrod, Cream City Review, Big Muddy, Quiddity*, and a host of other publications. Recent work has also received The Stanley Hanks Memorial Poetry Award from the St. Louis Poetry Center.

AMIE HEASLEY received her MFA in fiction from Western Michigan University in 2006. Most recently, her work has appeared online at *The Boiler Journal, Corium, Juked, The Smoking Poet*, and *Prick of the Spindle*. When she isn't writing fiction or creative nonfiction, she works as a freelance writer for the marketing and advertising industry. She, along with her beloved husband, daughter, and dog, calls Kalamazoo, Michigan, home.

TYLER HOLMAN, an award-winning artist with honors, graduates Lakeland College in May 2014. He'll receive a Bachelor of Arts degree with a double major in studio arts and graphic arts. With this batch of college-related exposure, he plans to use his degree to its greatest potential. Because of Tyler's dedication and skill that involves an assortment of artistic essentials, he was declared Lakeland College's most outstanding artist of 2014.

SALLY HOUTMAN is an expat American who currently lives in Wellington, New Zealand. She is the author of a nonfiction book and began writing fiction and poetry in 2007. Since that time, her work has appeared in more than thirty print and online publications, received four New Zealand writing awards, and been nominated for a Pushcart Prize.

RICH IVES has received numerous grants for his work in poetry, fiction, editing, publishing, translation and photography. His writing has appeared in *Verse, North American Review, Dublin Quarterly, Massachusetts Review, Northwest Review, Quarterly West, Iowa Review, Poetry Northwest, Virginia Quarterly Review, Fiction Daily*, and many more. He is the 2009 winner of the Francis Locke Memorial Poetry Award from *Bitter Oleander*. In 2011, he received a nomination for The Best of the Web and two nominations for both the Pushcart Prize and The Best of the Net. He is the 2012 winner of the Creative Nonfiction Prize from *Thin Air* magazine. His book of days, *Tunneling to the Moon*, was serialized with a work per day appearing for all of 2013 at http://silencedpress.com.

WILLIAM JENSEN grew up in Arizona and now lives in Texas. His work has appeared in *New Plains Review, Texas Review*, and elsewhere. He is the editor of *Southwestern American Literature* and *Texas Books in Review*. He is currently working on a novel.

LEE KISLING is a retired engineer and full-time student in creative writing at Hamline University in St. Paul, Minnesota. His first novel, *The Fools' War*, was published by HarperCollins Children's Books in 1992. A collection of his poems, *The Lemon Bars of Parnassus*, was recently published by Parallel Press.

Poet and essayist SANDRA KLEVEN is the editor of *Cirque*, a literary journal. Her work has been published in journals and anthologies including *Alaska Quarterly Review, Stoneboat, Oklahoma Review, F Magazine*, and *Cold Flashes*. It is collected in *Defiance Street: Poems and other writing* (Vered Publishing & Design House, 2013). Several pieces in the collections were nominated for the Pushcart Prize. Kleven has an MFA in creative writing from the University of Alaska Anchorage. Originally from Washington state, she has spent most of the last thirty years working in Alaska's village communities.

ZACHARY KLUCKMAN is a Pushcart Prize nominee and recipient of the Red Mountain Press National Poetry Prize, with work appearing in print globally. Featured on over 500 radio stations, he is an accomplished spoken word artist who has represented Albuquerque, New Mexico at both the National and Individual World Poetry Slams. He is the Spoken Word Editor for *The Pedestal*. His first collection, *Animals In Our Flesh*, was published in 2012 by Red Mountain Press and his new collection, *Some of It is Muscle*, was released in December 2013.

SUSANNA LANG's newest collection of poems, *Tracing the Lines*, was published in 2013 by Brick Road Poetry Press. Her first collection, *Even Now*, was published in 2008 by The Backwaters Press, and a chapbook, *Two by Two*, was released in 2011 from Finishing Line Press. She has published original poems and essays, and translations from the French, in such journals as *Little Star, New Letters, The Sow's Ear Poetry*

Review, Green Mountains Review, Baltimore Review, Kalliope, Southern Poetry Review, World Literature Today, Chicago Review, New Directions, and *Jubilat*. Translations include *Words in Stone* and *The Origin of Language*, both by Yves Bonnefoy. She lives in Chicago, where she teaches in the Chicago Public Schools.

EMILIE LINDEMANN is an assistant professor of English at Silver Lake College of the Holy Family in Manitowoc, Wisconsin. She is the author of *Dear Minimum Wage Employee* and *The Queen of the Milky Way* (both from dancing girl press). She is currently at work on an inter-arts collaboration called *Performance Anxiety* that will be coming to a stage or café near you. In her free time, Emilie plays violin with the folk rock band Cato Falls.

S. FREDERIC LISS has published or has forthcoming twenty-eight short stories and has received numerous awards and other forms of recognition for his short fiction. Liss has been published in *South Dakota Review, The South Carolina Review, Dogwood, The Worcester Review*, and *Fifth Wednesday Journal*, among others. In addition, he has written two collections of short stories, one of which was a finalist for the Flannery O'Connor Short Fiction Prize sponsored by University of Georgia Press and the other of which was a finalist in the Bakeless Prize Competition sponsored by Middlebury College and Bread Loaf Writers' Conference. Liss earned his MFA from Emerson College and was the recipient of a Grant-in-Aid in Literature from the St. Botolph Club Foundation in Boston, where he leads a workshop in writing fiction.

AL MAGINNES is the author of five full-length collections, most recently *Inventing Constellations* (Cherry Grove Edition, 2012) and *Ghost Alphabet* (White Pine Press, 2008). He is also winner of the White Pine Poetry Prize. He has new or forthcoming poems in *Georgia Review, Conte, Arkansas Review, Cave Wall, Chautauqua, Southern Humanities Review*, and others. He lives with his family in Raleigh, North Carolina and teaches composition, literature and creative writing at Wake Technical Community College.

JOHN MALONEY is a stonemason on Martha's Vineyard. He has published poems in *Poetry, Poetry Northwest, Ploughshares, Fulcrum, Agni online, Zoland Poetry Annual*, and *The New York Times* op-ed page. A book of poems, *Proposal*, was published by Zoland Books in 1999. Two poems are included in *The Book of Irish American Poetry: From the Eighteenth Century to the Present* (University of Notre Dame Press, 2007). A poem, "After Work," was Column 184 of *American Life in Poetry*.

JENNIFER MARTELLI was born and raised in Massachusetts and graduated from Boston University and The Warren Wilson MFA Program for Writers. She's taught high school English as well as women's literature at Emerson College in Boston. Her work has appeared or is forthcoming in *Denver Quarterly, Folio, Calliope, Kalliope, Mississippi Review, Bellingham Review, Kindred, Bitterzoet, ZigZag Folio, The Inflectionist Review, Sugared Water, Slippery Elm*, and *Tar River Review*. She was a finalist for the Sue Elkind Poetry Prize and a recipient of the Massachusetts Cultural Council Grant in Poetry. Her chapbook, *Apostrophe*, was published in 2011 by BigTable Publishing Company. She is currently at home with her two kids, is involved in the poetry scene in Salem, Massachusetts, and teaches occasional classes at the Peabody Library.

JOHN McCARTHY's work has appeared or is forthcoming in *The Pinch, Salamander, Oyez Review, Midwestern Gothic, Jabberwock Review, SPECS, Digital Americana, The Conium Review*, and *The Lindenwood Review*, among others. He lives in Springfield, Illinois where he is the Assistant Editor of *Quiddity*.

REBECCA MEYER was born in Chicago and grew up in Wausau, Wisconsin. She has degrees in writing and Spanish from Lakeland College. Rebecca currently resides in Wausau, working in an elementary school as a Spanish paraprofessional.

The poetry, prose and artwork of ROBERT L. PENICK has appeared in over 100 different literary journals, including *North American Review*, *The Hudson Review*, and *The California Quarterly*. He serves as Deputy Circuit Court Clerk in Louisville, Kentucky and lives with his turtle, Sheldon.

CHARLES RAFFERTY has published poems in *The New Yorker*, *Prairie Schooner*, and *The Southern Review*. In 2009, he received a creative writing fellowship from the NEA. A book of poems, *The Unleashable Dog*, is forthcoming from Steel Toe Books. His collection of short fiction, *Saturday Night at Magellan's*, was published by Fomite Press in 2013. Currently, he directs the MFA program at Albertus Magnus College.

WILEY READING is a twenty-something non-profit goon living and working in D.C. She would like to thank her long career in public school for the opportunities it gave her to develop her drawing skills— there was just no other way than drawing to survive endless lectures on Nathaniel Hawthorne and the Pythagorean theorem. Wiley is a regular contributor at *Disrupting Dinner Parties*.

JULIA RICE likes to grapple with reality in the field of poetry. After half a life spent teaching high school English and half a life practicing law in Chicago, she picked up her pen, moved to the Burnham Park neighborhood in Milwaukee, and became a member of the Wisconsin Fellowship of Poets, Greenleaf Writers, and Urban Echo poets. She is also a Franciscan sister. Her poetry has appeared in the WFOP *Museletter*, *2014 Wisconsin Poets Calendar*, *Songs of St. Francis*, *Echolocations: Poets Map Madison*, *Alive Now*, *The Goose River Anthology 2013*, and *WildaMorrisBlogspot*, and will appear in *Soundings Review* and the *2015 Poets Calendar*.

W. JACK SAVAGE is a retired broadcaster and educator. He is the author of six books: three novels, two short story collections, and the autobiographical *The High Sky of Winter's Shadows* (wjacksavage.com). More than a hundred of Jack's stories and drawings have been published worldwide. Jack and his wife Kathy live in Monrovia, California.

PETER SCHALLER is an artist and activist who lives and works in Nicaragua. He works for Rayo de Sol, a small community development organization. His free time is dedicated to writing, photography and promoting environmental awareness. He is at work on a collection of essays, poetry and photographs entitled *After the Silence*.

MARVIN SHACKELFORD holds an MFA from the University of Montana. His work appears in such journals as *Confrontation*, *Beloit Fiction Journal*, *burntdistrict*, and *Armchair/Shotgun*. He lives in Texas, earning a living in agriculture. Tweets @WorderFarmer.

DANNY EARL SIMMONS is an Oregonian and a proud graduate of Corvallis High School. He is a friend of the Linn-Benton Community College Poetry Club and an active member of Albany Civic Theater. His poems have appeared in a variety of journals such as *The Pedestal Magazine*, *Naugatuck River Review*, *Off the Coast*, *IthacaLit*, and *Fifth Wednesday Journal*.

JEANINE STEVENS studied poetry at UC Davis and has her MA from California State University. She has seven chapbooks and is the author of *Sailing on Milkweed* (WordTech Communications, 2012). Her work has appeared in *Poet Lore*, *Evansville Review*, *Harpur Palate*, *Pearl*, and *South Dakota Review*. She is the 2013 recipient of the MacGuffin Poet Hunt judged by Philip Levine. Jeanine also creates collages that reflect many of her poems. She is a member of the Squaw Valley Community of Writers. An Indiana native, she now lives in Sacramento and Lake Tahoe.

LOREN SUNDLEE's poems have appeared in a variety of magazines and journals, including *Bellowing Ark, River Oak Review, Talking River Review*, and *Windfall*. A chapbook of his poems, *Looking Both Ways*, was published in 2012. Raised in western Minnesota, he now lives in central Washington.

KAZ SUSSMAN is a curmudgeon, fortunately ensnared by the full moon. He is a carpenter and disaster response worker, and he lives in a home he has built in Oregon from abandoned poems. His work has appeared or is forthcoming in *Raven Chronicles, Nimrod International Journal, Bacopa Literary Review, Dos Passos Review, Whitefish Review, The Misfit Journal*, and *Gastronomica*, among other publications. Find him online at www.kazsussman.com.

CINDY VEACH manages fundraising programs for nonprofit organizations. Her poetry has appeared in *Chelsea, Prairie Schooner, Chicago Review, Carolina Quarterly, Poet Lore, WomenArts Quarterly Journal, Weave Magazine, Sou'wester*, and others, and she has work forthcoming in *Midwest Quarterly, Paterson Literary Review, Connotation Press*, and *Crab Creek Review*. She was a finalist for the Ann Stanford Prize and the recipient of an honorable mention in the Ratner-Ferber-Poet Lore Prize and the *Crab Creek Review* Poetry Prize. She lives in Manchester, Massachusetts.

ROBERT VIVIAN is the author of *The Tall Grass Trilogy, Water and Abandon*, and two books of meditative essays. He's currently at work on a collection of dervish essays.

DAVID WALKER teaches and is the founding editor of *Golden Walkman Magazine*, a literary magazine in the form of a podcast. His fiction and poetry appears or is forthcoming in *Words Dance, Cactus Heart, MadHat, Diversion Press, Paper Nautilus*, and others. He can always be contacted at dwalker8508@yahoo.com.

TIMOTHY WALSH's most recent poetry collection is *When the World Was Rear-Wheel Drive: New Jersey Poems* (Main Street Rag Publishing). His awards include the Grand Prize in the Atlanta Review International Poetry Competition, the Kurt Vonnegut Fiction Prize from *North American Review*, and the Wisconsin Academy Fiction Prize. He is the author of a book of literary criticism, *The Dark Matter of Words: Absence, Unknowing, and Emptiness in Literature* (Southern Illinois University Press) and two other poetry collections, *Wild Apples* (Parallel Press) and *Blue Lace Colander* (Marsh River Editions). Find more at timothyawalsh.com.

SAM WILDER was raised in Marietta, Ohio and Boone, North Carolina. He received his MFA in fiction from American University in Washington, D.C. in 2012. He now lives and writes in Chicago.

MEEAH WILLIAMS is a writer and graphic artist. Her work has appeared or is forthcoming in the journals *Meat for Tea, Offcourse, The Milo Review, Dead Flowers*, and *Petrichor Review*, among others. She lives in Brooklyn, New York with her husband Hank.

MÜESSER YENIAY was born in Izmir, Turkey, and graduated from Ege University with a degree in English Language and Literature. She has won several prizes in Turkey including Yunus Emre (2006), Homeros Attila İlhan (2007), Ali Riza Ertan (2009), and Enver Gökçe (2013). Her work has been published in many books, collections, and magazines, and her poems have been translated into ten languages. She is editor of the poetry magazine *Şiirden*. She is pursuing a PhD in Turkish literature at Bilkent University, Ankara, and is also a member of PEN and the Writers Syndicate of Turkey.

Editorial Focus

Stoneboat is an independent biannual journal of literature and arts that is dedicated to publishing quality fiction, nonfiction, memoir, poetry, artwork, and graphic literature. We strive to showcase outstanding and diverse work from both emerging and established artists. Ours is a larger format publication compared to traditional journals since we believe in giving contributors' work room to breathe.

www.ingramcontent.com/pod-product-compliance
Lightning Source LLC
Chambersburg PA
CBHW081205170626
46813CB00010B/3329